HUMANITY

Every Child lifeline / DEMO GOG international magazine

Vietnamese Russian Serbian Unions of Writers (28-39)

Author Tamikio L Dooley
And her contribution to Choism
(73)

Poetry Clinic (42-49)

CUGA* (14-19)

August 2023 issue

*Writers Union of North America

Every Child lifeline / DEMO GOG international magazine

Lucilla Trapazzo
EUROPE

Every Child lifeline /DEMO GOG international magazine

Face of the continent

Lucilla Trapazzo

is a Swiss/Italian poet, translator, artist and performer. After years spent abroad, for studies and work, in the DDR, Brussels, Washington DC and NYC, she now lives in Zurich, Switzerland. Convinced supporter of human rights and the planet, her social and feminine point of view is reflected in many of her writings.

Five her books of poetry

Editor of the poetry section of MockUp Magazine, Italy and of Innsaei Literary Journal, India, co-editor of several international anthologies, Lucilla Trapazzo is a juror in international poetry competitions, and has co-organized and moderated poetry events, International Festivals and art exhibitions for International associations. She is a frequent guest at numerous International festivals (including Struga Poetry Evenings 2021, N. Macedonia; Princeton 2021 USA; and Babylon International Festival of the Arts 2022, Baghdad).
Her poems have been translated into 18 languages and extensively published in International literary magazines and anthologies. Numerous are the awards and the recognitions worldwide (just a few: first prize best poetry book "I Murazzi" Torino 2019; first prize Civil and Philosophical Poems, XI Checkhov's Autumn International Festival, Crimea 2021; Creativity Award Naji Naaman, Lebanon 2021; Best Book of the Year, "4th Bo'ao International Poetry Festival" for Ruscellante, People Republic of China 2021; First prize for Peace and Social Justice, Centro Studi Cultura e Società, Torino 2022; Silke Liria Award for poetic expression at Ditët e Naimit International Poetry Festival, Tetovo, N.Macedonia 2022; poet laureate Kurora e Poezisë, Korca International Festival Netët të Poezisë, Albania 2023.

From one of her poems, Salmodia, which tells of a child bride, a video was made (Palazzo del Poeta production, OST Marco Di Stefano), broadcasted by Italian National TV RAI 1 in the spring and autumn seasons in 2021.

Beyond the gaze

Shattering is the misery of an injury
bound to libations of silence.
Mournful sum of time and space,
returns the migrant mother of the son
crucified to the disdain of crows
and torn apart between night and day
without ending nor beginning. Inhabiting
streets and houses abandoned to the memories,
in the magazines appear only photograms
or distracted words of news bulletins
in the evening on TV - just hollow noises
and frills of conscience in dissonance.
Sweet denial follows compassion.

Ego absolvo te a peccatis mundi. *

*(Latin – Catholic formula to absolve sinners)

Oltre lo sguardo

*Urlante è la miseria di uno squarcio
avvinto a libagioni di silenzio.
Somma dolente d'ogni tempo e luogo
torna migrante la madre del figlio
al ludibrio dei corvi crocifisso
dilaniato tra notte e giorno senza
fine e inizio. Abitando le strade
e case abbandonate alla memoria
nei rotocalchi solo fotogrammi
parole di distratti notiziari
la sera alla TV, vacuo frastuono
e orpelli di coscienza in dissonanza.
Dolce il diniego segue compassione.*

Ego absolvo te a peccatis mundi.

Every Child lifeline /DEMO GOG international magazine

Free microphone

*

on my black hair
Pomegranate flowers have grown
This autumn smells like spring

*

This time freedom
from my hair
will rise
oh wind
twist my hair

Bullet

This time
All the boundaries of my body belong to you
Shoot
Shoot
My hair waves in the wind
It will drown you
bullet
bullets
We are afraid
in our wounds
We have buried
the freedom
i kiss your lips

*

in my eyes
deer
for peace
He will run through a passage full of mines
Maybe this explosion
The end of all wars.

Sanaz Davoodzadehfar (Iran) Sanaz Davoodzadehfar is an Iranian poet born in Iran and living in Luxembourg . She began her artistic career with theatre and worked in many plays winning many awards in this field . She worked on storytelling for children and began to learn from traditional Iranian songs .She is a student of Pari maleki and Mojtaba asgari ,the great musicians of traditional music in Iran. She began writing poetry in classical forms .Her poems were published in the most important Iranian journals and newspapers and sites like: roudaki,zane emeooz,piadehro,neveshta,... Many of her poems were translated into other languages such as English, French, Spanish, German, Swedish, Kurdish. Her first collection " I walk on dead letters" was translated into Arabic and published in Tamoz publishing in Syria.It is the first collection of poetry translated into Arabic from the works pf a woman Iranian poet after Forough Farrokhzad who had a very successful presence in the most important exhibitions of the Arabic book, such as Beirut, Cairo, Muscat, Baghdad ... Most of her poems were published in the most important Arabic newspapers and websites, such as Al-Ahram, Al-Dustour, Al-Adab,Al-Hayat and ... Many critics of Arab wrote positive reviews of her collection in newspapers, magazines and critique books. _She has participated in many Arabic and global festivals and poetry such as Iraq, Oman, Tunisia ,Romania .... A Poetry collection containing poems by three female poets from Iran published in Czechoslovakia with Radek Hassliki and Sanaz was one of them. -Her poetry collection was translated and published in the language of Amaziqi, translated by Mazzak Eidar in Morocco. Her poetry collection is available in Spanish, translated by Tive Martinez in Spain.Her second and latest poetry collection published in Tehran reached the finals in the poetry award in Iran.Her first poetry collection was translated to Romanian recently and her collection won the first prize in poetry in European poetry .A champion in romania and won Alhawaheri prize in Sydney, Australia.

Every Child lifeline /DEMO GOG international magazine

Free microphone

FROM SOKOLOVTSI TO ROZHEN
(from low to high)

On the path
between
the pines
a stream
follows
the Top -
To touch
the primroses
and to make cry
the soil.

TRAVELLING

Unreal houses
from childhood
searching in the night
pilgrims.
Raindrops
reverberate
in someone's
slumbering chimney.
They get angry -
 the ancient rebels.
They are waiting in ambush
the rainbow - to pass
  over the days
  and to remain.
In the snow.

THE SOARING MAN

                  Vasil's, my brother

Blue.
Purple.
The pier...
The time
get used to lonely.
Pink.
Yellow.
Without her.
I shake
of sky
from the eye.
Sandy.
Wild.
Foretell.
And the eyes
become impoverished.
The shadows –
makeup
and greatness.
In the wake of
the moon –
a wanderer.

Rozalia Aleksandrova lives in Plovdiv, Bulgaria. She was born in the magical Rhodope Mountains, the cradle of Orpheus. Author of 12 poetry books. Editor and compiler of over 30 literary almanacs, collections and anthologies. She is a member of the Union of Bulgarian Writers and member of Association of Plovdivs Writers. She is in the Board Directors of the site Atunis Galaxy Poetry. She is President for Bulgaria of UHE and Association Mill Mentes por Mexico International. She is an advisor of PLWV and Brand Ambasador of NLHF. She is Ambassador of Prodigy Life Academy US.

    Her poems was translated into many languages: Polish, English, Spanish, Bengali, Hindi, Farsi, Serbian, Italian, French, Arabic, Romanian, Albanian, Russian, Greek, Chinesse, Turkish. Her poems have been published in many prestigious collections, almanacs, literary magazines and websites in Bulgaria, Europe and the world. In March 2006 she created a poetic-intellectual association "Quantum and Friends" for the promotion of quantum poetry in civil society, Plovdiv and Bulgarian phenomenon. Initiator and chief organizer of the International Festival of Poetry SPIRITUALITY WITHOUT BORDERS from 2015.

    She is one of the winners of the prestigious CESAR VALLEJO Prize for Literature – 2022 and CESAR VALLEJO EXCELENCE Prize 2023 for Cultural Modality and too for Modality - Defense of Peace and social justice Prize. Winner of the MAHATMA GANDHI Leadership Award 2022, Awarded like Woman Leader in Transcedence Chapter Greece and others.

Every Child lifeline /DEMO GOG international magazine
Free microphone

Peace,
So expensive
We buy so many weapons
To maintain it

If we pray more
If we were kind to each other

We could say
We have Peace of mind
Poetic heart
Call for meditation
Inside our heart

Peace,
We say a lot
We make nothing

Peace,
Such as a woman
We adore
But few can get

Peace,
A value with no cost
If the humans understand the word...

I wish one day....

Eva Petropoulou Eva Lianou Petropoulou

Eva Lianou Petropoulou (Greece) She is an awarded author and poet from Greece with more than 25 years in the Literary field published more that 10 books. Her poems are translated in more than 15 languages. She is President of creativity and art of Mil Mentes Por Mexico Association represent Greece, President of Global UHE Peru, Vice President of Cultural Association China, Mexico.

Love

I wish i had a love
A love as it should be
No more take and take...

I wish I had a friend
As friends should be
Be close to hard times
Listen to our wishes
Support us

I wish i had met a person
That could understand me
Only from my eyes
Or my mood

But if i had all that
Maybe i would never write poems

Poetry is my path
Poetry is my strength

Eva Petropoulou Eva Lianou Petropoulou

I saw in the flames...
The crying faces of each branches
A big why???
Why you burn the trees???
Why you destroy your future

I saw in flames their tears...
I saw my face
So sad face
Why you burn the trees??

The birds don't sing
The animals
The fox
The wolves
The sheeps
The dogs
The horses
The cat

Have no voice anymore
Nobody has a voice

The flames take it away....

Eva Petropoulou Eva Lianou Petropoulou

Every Child lifeline /DEMO GOG international magazine

Free microphone

Bogdana Găgeanu is a poetess and a playwright . She has been published in anthologies and magazines. Her playwrights have been heard to different radios.She received a lot of international awards. She had many interviews with Loi Monroe,Gelda Castro,Helen Sarita,Dustin Pickering,Dennis Brown. She likes to inspire. She wrote her first book of poems,"My soul pyramid ". She wrote a script for a short Romanian movie called "GPS"

Deaf-mute

A deaf mute is trying
To express with his body language
What the mouth can 't utter.
He was forced to compose
A new language of commmunication
To reach to others.
What do we see when he is talking?
Only signs or a new speaking web?

Ego

Ego can make a human being
Feel superior
The human being is having
Many ,many floors
Because of ego.
The level of watching is more higher
Than the usual one.
It Is better to have fear of heights.

Bogdana Găgeanu

Every Child lifeline /DEMO GOG international magazine

Free microphone

Untold Words

What I didn't get to say
is still waiting for you
hermetically sealed,
sealed by my longing
that maybe they will see the light,
refuse the silence
that had condemned them for years
and become encouraged
prepared to be led to you,
to caress the lips,
to thrust through,
to hide nothing,
to surrender,
to endure.
What will become of them?
No one knows...
...you might drive them away,
maybe you'll mock them.
Keep them inside you forever:
That's what I'd like.
And if you throw them away, don't...
Give them back to me,
They're mine.
I'll pick them up
even if I'm alone.
Like I've been doing all this time,
I'll love you in my solitude...

Sanctuary

There are secrets that no one knows,
dark oceans in the deepest depths of the mind
that you have not discovered so far.
It is the breaths that seek union with the divine,
two bodies,
one idea,
infinite light of love.
Sparkles of magic sensing the desire
to break silences,
to break chains,
to sail into the sacred sanctum of the soul
until the resonance of redemption is revealed,
with a clear destiny to listen to
small and great truths
in your deep, troubled waters
until they arise to the touch of the sun
parts of the sea
that flood the whole being.
If the eyes are born again,
if silences are broken,
if secrets are revealed,
and hurricanes are hushed,
then hearts will beat loudly
like thunder,
fears will be tamed
like pitch black
wild horses!

BIOGRAPHY
Antonis Filippeos was born in Athens in 1980. He had been to Italy for two years for studies in the university of Rome. Returning to Greece, he completed his studies in International and European Relations in Athens and he obtained his degree in Italian Literature at university of Athens in 2012.
With his inexhaustible creativity, he managed to set in the field of poetry. His first book, "Animus Nudus"(Cactus publications), was well reviewed and he won a lot of international awards.
Some of his poems were set to music and translated in English, Italian and Russian. Lots of his poems have been included in various poetic anthologies and famous magazines. His promising second brand-new book "Silentium" (Cactus publications) has been recently published.

Every Child lifeline /DEMO GOG international magazine

Free microphone

HYPERPOEM POETRY

Unparalleled Poetry

Humanity bonding through ink
Your words and mine interlinked
Poetry pushing the boundaries
Ever increasing in its global unity
Record breaking in its length
Peace and togetherness its ultimate goal
Organised, overseen by the talented Alexander Kabishev
Efforts forged to maintain a togetherness
Messages of peace in a troubled world.
Donna McCabe ©

Climb The Mountain...

Scaling the mountain of life
Facing fears, pitfalls and slippery slopes
Yet broadening horizons along the way
Fuelling the want and need to grow
Finding strength and courage to climb on
To survey your own personal vista.
Donna McCabe ©

A Woman Of Substance

Worldly and knowledgable
Open and caring
Many a role she has to fulfil
A strong constitution, yet soft underneath
Nurturer of new life
Holder of family bond's, ties and connections
Openly sharing her love
Offering the knowledge she knows
Devoted and loving too the end.
Donna McCabe ©

On Reading...

Looking for knowledge
Wanting to soak it all in
Universal, spiritual,
Everything that's akin
Needing to know things
The deeper meaning of it all
Yet time is the enemy
I can never forestall
So I'll never know everything
This is for sure
But the pleasure of reading
I know has many a cure.
Donna McCabe ©

Prognosticate

Predictions foretold
Readings of many kinds
Outguessing the odds
Gauging the outcome of events
Needing to know the outcome
Omens of good and bad
Signals given from all around
To make known in advance
Indications of what lays ahead
Calculating the bonuses of this
Anticipating what will happen
The future is being read
Evaluating all the pros and cons.
Donna McCabe ©

Biography of Donna McCabe

She is an experienced poet with over twenty years of experience whose vast variety of work has gained her multiple accolades within her field of literature over the years. She has been published both nationally and internationally in journals, magazines and anthologies as well as reviewing them too. She is a highly respected admin in multiple social media groups, and is a regular contributor to literature. Besides this she is an artist also. Her intricate wordplay displayed in her works has been personified by her past and concurrent experiences which include her hardships, trials and tribulations. Her lifetime admiration of reading and writing and love of art has steered her into an adventurous new direction of collaborations with an up -and- coming Canadian artist Ala Ilescu whose idiosyncratic mind and artistic works compliment the vivid images her narrative works paint. These collaborations have resulted in a beautiful book of poetry and artwork entitled "Explosion Of Love" published on Amazon. Her creativity has also taken her onto other platforms in recent times, using Instagram to reach out and display her love of writing, artwork and love of the natural world to a wider audience. Her writings and interactions with the wider poetry communities there have helped her gain a good following and many awards and features too.

Instagram: @donnamccabe_

Facebook: Poemsbydonnamccabe

Every Child lifeline /DEMO GOG international magazine

Free microphone

Italy /Sicily /Sciacca.
Maria Nicol Metz
In the heart the silence of age

Two hearts
on a bench
next to them
the noises
of a city on the move
but their eyes
they were captivated
from the surrounding beauties.
Around their lives
the caresses of the wind
in the heart the silence of age
close to the memories of life
many sighs inside dreams
hand in hand
love was
the mirror of time.

©Copyright Francesco Favetta
Maria
Maria Nicol Metz
The eternal spouse of life

I have to go
it is no longer possible
stay
within these walls
what freedom
he is in jail
and every breath
underlies
to the windows of deception.
Time again
the eternal spouse of life
that scans
seasons
and the song of hope
in inner silence
like a sleepless cross
stripped of evil
scatters his seed in the world.

©Copyright Francesco Favetta

The poet Francesco Favetta was born in Sicily in Sciacca, he has always loved poetry, writing verses, but above all culture, true culture, food for the soul!

So far he has written more than 4000 poems, he also writes philosophical reflections and thoughts.

In 2018, he was awarded and awarded by the Academy of Sicily:

Academician of Sicily.

Free microphone

Every Child lifeline / NEMO

Duška Kontić rođena u Zenici 1958.godine. Osnovnu i srednju školu završila je u Nikšiću. Diplomirala je na Filozofskom fakultetu u Nikšiću na odsjeku za srpskohrvatski jezik i jugoslovensku književnost. Dugi niz godina je službovala u Telekomu, a ostvarila se i u profesorskom pozivu u Osnovnoj školi ,,Jagoš Kontić" u Nikšiću. Pisanjem se bavi još od djetinjstva. Član je Književne zajednice ,,Mirko Banjević" iz Nikšića u okviru koje je izdala zbirku poezije ,, Nemirni smiraj". Takođe je član Međunarodnog udruženja književnih stvaralaca i umjetnika ,,Nekazano" iz Bara i udruženja književnika i umjetnika "Zenit" iz Podgorice sa kojima ima uspešnu sinergiju. Sarađivala je u mnogim zbornicima i časopisima u regionu u okviru kojih su zastupljene njene pjesme. Pjesme su joj objavljivane u antologijama širom svijeta. Živi u Nikšiću, država Crna Gora. Ostvarena

Za Magazine Himanity

Bučna tišina

Tišina je bojila zidove i pravila rezove na njenom licu, u jednom trenutku njeno lice se raspalo u milion staklastih krhotina...sakupila je stakliće i napravila novu sebe, sretniju, pametniju.

Odlučila je da ode u nepokorene, nepoznate svjetove. U zatvorena vrata zarila je nož i rekla zbogom starom načinu života. Teško je donijela odluku. Ostavila je porodicu, spakovala svoje bitisanje u mali, bolni kofer uzdisaja, da prigrli tišinu, da se odmori, da pokuša da preživi pakao koji je urnisao danima. Drugačije nije moglo, tiranin se smijao, nije vidio njenu zgužvanu bluzu natopljenu suzama. Teško su prolazili dani u očajanju, preispitivanjima i želji da makar na tren vidi svoju djecu. Tišina je bila nepodnošljiva, jača od grmljavine, zasljepljujuće munje su parale izmoreni um i ranjeno srce. Strahovi su krstarili njenom utrobom, bol do bola se nizao, lomio je, krio se u kofere, pa nenadadano iizlazio, raspomamljen. Dugi dani su tražili ishodište, plakalo je napušteno ognjište, nije imala gdje da se vrati, previše mjesta su uzeli sunovrati neprospavanih noći. Pijanstvo partnera i njena nemoć da ispravi greške i sačuva porodicu rađale su ranjenu rimu u njenim mislima. Puste odaje su ječale neprebolom. Suze su se sudarale u nijemim prostorijama i kitile nemoćne grudi koje su se nadimale pod teretom tuge. Nepodnošljiva, samotna, beskrajna noć, ulivala se u krike tišine, nesavladiva tuga je kropila pretkomore srca i gasila snove. Da li je bila ljubav, kako se sve odjednom promijenilo, zašto je čovjek za koga bi učinila sve postao neumoljivi stranac, pitala se u dugim, predugim satima kroz ubode trome kazaljke. Pitanja bez odgovora bubnjala su u njenoj glavi, stihovi su sami od sebe počeli da teku.

Od muke, iz bola, rima se udizala i osvjetljavala mračne staze, putokazi su se otvarali i vodili je u ljepotu riječi. Posvetila se pjesmi, duhovnom odrastanju uz promisao Boga. Iz njene duše emanirao je tužan stih, stvorila je najljepše balade koje su čitali ljudi iz cijelog svijeta.

Duška Kontić, Nikšić

Every Child lifeline /DEMO GOG international magazine

Free microphone

WITH A CHILD'S EYES

I want to see the world with a child's eyes
almond-shaped, clear, limpid, and innocent:
a meadow where people and flowers grow,
where hunger, poverty, and evil are absent.

I want to see the world with a child's eyes,
feel caressed by my dreams' incantation,
be able to touch the horizon with one hand
and reach the stars using only a ladder.

I don't want to see the world with my own
eyes. They've seen too much, they see the
universe behind a thick permanent haze.
Immersed in tears that never dry.

A DANGER

We are threatened by a great danger,
it's not an atomic bomb that destroys
all; it erodes the serenity and peace and
fills it with sadness, removes the words.

Loneliness—the lack of affection—
has created a spider's web in the soul,
while selfishness, vanity, fears,
and prejudices suffocate this world.

It's time to take off all the masks,
those that carry them for a lifetime,
then, the youth who recently use them
learning to live with hypocrisy, thus.

We are threatened by a great danger...

UNDER THE DARK SKY

I was looking up at the dark sky,
for so long I gazed at the stars,
as eyes in love they caressed me,
a lot of prayers burned inside of me.

Suddenly in my thoughts found space
for the many sufferings of this world,
of those who wake up with arms
or those who die under hunger's claw.

My body became soundless and light,
the sorrows diminished in a flash,
there're so many pains that mine
are insignificant in the universe.

And hence, my prayers expanded
under that dark and starry sky.

Irma Kurti is an Albanian poet, writer, lyricist, journalist, and translator and has been writing since she was a child. She is a naturalized Italian and lives in Bergamo, Italy. All her books are dedicated to the memory of her beloved parents, Hasan Kurti and Sherife Mezini, who have supported and encouraged every step of her literary path.

Irma Kurti has won numerous literary prizes and awards in Italy and Italian Switzerland. She was awarded the Universum Donna International Prize IX Edition 2013 for Literature and received a lifetime nomination as an Ambassador of Peace by the University of Peace, Italian Switzerland. In 2020, she became the honorary president of WikiPoesia, the encyclopedia of poetry.

She is a member of the jury for several literary competitions in Italy. She is also a translator for the *Ithaca* Foundation in Spain.

Irma Kurti has published 26 books in Albanian, 22 in Italian, 15 in English, and two in French. She has written approximately 150 lyrics for adults and children. She has also translated 16 books by different authors, and all of her own books into Italian and English. She is one of the most translated and published Albanian poets. Her books have been published in the United States, Canada, France, Italy, Netherlands, Belgium, Romania, Turkey, Kosovo, the Philippines, Cameroon, India, Chile, and Serbia.

Every Child lifeline /DEMO GOG international magazine

Free microphone

Mitar Stojković - "Little Prince" of the contemporary Serbian art scene

Behind the art brand Mitar Art is a dedicated artist. Or rather, a self-aware and refined artistic mind who stands firm, thinking through the world around him with a brush, and filling its essence with colors.

Mitar Stojković was born in 1978. He initially started making art as a boy through drawing. And indeed, the influence of good drawing is evident on his canvases. Nevertheless, over time he turned to other techniques, without fear of experimenting, like an eternally curious boy - the "Little Prince" of the contemporary Serbian art scene. He perceives art as freedom, and the creative process as a process of liberation.

His canvases are dominated by characters from movies, comics, Serbian Orthodox history, landscapes, animals, ordinary people... And regardless of the topic he works on, he approaches it with the same seriousness and dedication until he achieves artistic perfection.

Paintings that display recognizable and less recognizable characters seem as if they were created for large murals that would beautify the walls of the city center. Although they have clear lines and shapes, these drawings transferred into painter's canvases exude a special emotion and correspond very easily with the observer.

His artistic curiosity is not only directed towards portraiture. His canvases are also a tribute to the expressionist landscape. This shows artistic and craft diversity and the courage to try different motifs and directions.

His landscapes and abstractions are also very refined and extravagant, with a very interesting choice of colors, which makes his painting recognizable and his brand a serious contender for a special place in the contemporary Serbian artistic scene.

Text by Ana Stjelja
If you want to choose his paintings, you can find more on his Instagram
https://instagram.com/mitar.art.8?igshid=NjIwNzIyMDk2Mg==

Every Child lifeline /DEMO GOG international magazine

СПСА—Натали Биссо

ЧТО ТАКОЕ МЛАТТ

Приветствую новых читателей и тех, кто уже знаком с замечательным, красочным, очень грамотно и красиво оформленным, и отредактированным международным журналом HUMANITY, редактором которого является молодой талантливый писатель, активист и организатор многих проектов, основатель великолепного проекта ГИПЕРПОЭМА, Александр Кабишев.

Отрадно, что наше сотрудничество не только продолжается, но крепнет день ото дня. И я всегда бесконечно рада встречам с читателями журнала HUMANITY во всех странах мира.
Мне хотелось бы представить несколько ярких личностей и их творчество, а так же рассказать о Международной Литературной Ассоциации "Творческая Трибуна"(МЛАТТ)/ International Literary Association "Creative Tribune" (ILACT).

На фоне международной нестабильности в политике, экономике, отношений между странами и народами, поэты, писатели, люди культуры и искусства, вся творческая интеллигенция чувствуют себя в крайне уязвимом положении. По многим аспектам есть или появились разного рода ограничения в общении, в обмене культурными ценностями, в сотрудничестве, в поездках. Но душа писателя, она не может сидеть взаперти, ей необходима свобода, полёт не только мысли, но и слова, полёт души в конце концов, для написания хороших прозаических произведений, стихов, песен.

С другой стороны, интернет предоставляет, (хоть и ограниченную), возможность для общения между творческими людьми. На этом фоне все ресурсы интернетных сетей стали пестрить невероятным количеством разного рода мероприятий, конкурсов, конференций, и само собой Дипломов(в том числе и фейковых). Хотелось бы предостеречь уважаемых авторов, как состоявшихся, так и молодых, начинающих, неискушенных, что бы они тщательнее и внимательнее относились к выбору мероприятий, в которых принимают участие.

К великому сожалению среди действительно грамотно организованных проектов, конкурсов и фестивалей юридически существующими творческими объединениями, Союзами писателей, Ассоциациями, Академиями, с подбором профессионального Жюри в своих областях, появилось множество фейковых "организаций, объединений и даже так называемых "Академий", которыми правит один человек во всевозможных ипостасях, который жаждет признания, славы и известности.

На фоне всех этих факторов Международная Литературная Ассоциация "Творческая Трибуна" выглядит тихой гаванью настоящего творца. Но она самым активным и ответственным образом ведёт подготовку каждого отдельного проекта.

Ассоциация не хватает за горло автора, она предлагает редкие и интересные проекты. Она тщательным образом продумывает, создаёт или приглашает в Жюри настоящих профессиональных мастеров своего дела. Ассоциация подняла планку проведения своих конкурсов на самый высокий уровень, точно по срокам соблюдая регламент проведения и подведения Итогов.

В президиуме Ассоциации состоят яркие, самобытные, талантливые, давно состоявшиеся в литературе и поэзии авторы, ответственные, опытные, нравственно устоявшиеся эстеты. И самое главное, это люди, которые готовы жертвовать своим драгоценным временем для дружбы и сплочения между писателя и поэтами, деятелями культуры и искусства всех стран мира. Литература и искусство наиболее ярким образом отзывается в сердцах людей на любом континенте, музыка понятна без слов, стихи на разных языках (в хороших переводах) проникают в души читателей и остаются в них навсегда, а иногда даже меняют судьбы людей - настолько велика сила слова.

Международная Литературная Ассоциация "Творческая Трибуна"(МЛАТТ) проводит литературные конкурсы на двух языках(русском и английском), оценивая и присуждая призовые места в равной степени на этих двух языках. Мультиязычные конкурсы, как никакие другие, привлекают участников со всего мира и тем самым вершат, в прямом смысле, объединение народов в дружную, высокоразвитую, интеллигентную семью, в которой, всё же, каждый автор - индивидуальность с большой буквы.

В то же время Литературная Ассоциация "Творческая Трибуна" не является конкурентом и не стремится сместить с орбиты авторитета и популярности никакой из творческих Союзов и объединений и занять чужое место на вершине холма, наоборот, шагая по просто-

Every Child lifeline /DEMO GOG international magazine

СПСА—Натали Биссо

рам международных литературы и искусств, готова сотрудничать с творческими коллективами на международном уровне, вести совместно новые проекты, укреплять дружбу и сотрудничество между творческой интеллигенцией. Именно так записано и в Уставе Ассоциации.

Так что, приглашаем к сотрудничеству, на благо процветания мира, дружбы, культуры и литературы на нашей голубой планете Земля. Тем более, что в нашей Ассоциации заняты такие замечательные и интересные творческие люди и настоящие Мастера своего дела, как Раиса Мельникова и Сария Маммадова, которых я и хотела бы сегодня представить.

Натали Биссо,
поэт, писатель, Академик, Президент МЛАТТ, Руководитель ГОСПСА.
Германия

НАТАЛИ БИССО - поэт, прозаик, эссеист, поэт-песенник. Автор 13 авторских сборников, соавтор в более 180 международных сборниках. Стихи переведены на 40 языков мира и опубликованы в международных антологиях.

Почётный Деятель Мировых литературы и искусств с присвоением серебряного знака. Принимает участие в литературной жизни разных стран.

Учредитель и Президент Международной Литературной Ассоциации "Творческая Трибуна"(МЛАТТ).

Академик International Academy for the Development of Literature and Art; Академик международной Академии русской словесности(МАРС); член-корреспондент Международной Академии Наук и Искусств(МАНИ).

Почетный Член WRITERS UNION OF NORTH AMERICA, руководитель Германского отделения СПСА, член Международного Союза Авторов и Исполнителей(МСАИ).

Член Cámara Internacional de Escritores & Artistas и Всемирного Совета CIESART (Испания). Член Интернационального Союза Писателей(ИСП), член Регионального Общественного Фонда содействия развитию современной поэзии "СВЕТОЧ", член Международной Гильдии Писателей(Германия), Член Международной Ассоциации Писателей и Публицистов, Член Евразийской творческой гильдии (Лондон).

Советник международного издания китайской литературы(Федерации литературных и художественных кругов Хубэй), член Жюри международных конкурсов, Посол Международного форума творчества и человечности(IFCH)(Morokko), Член Европейского совета и Межконтинентального консультативного комитета RINASCIMENTO-RENAISSANCE Millennium III(Египет); Почетный Президент „Thousand Minds for Mexico" и международного жюри в Германии (Мексика), Почётный член Союза испаноязычных Писателей (UXE).

Многократный Гран-Призёр и Лауреат международных литературных и музыкальных конкурсов; обладатель нескольких специальных международных премий - получила более 400 дипломов лауреата; многократный Кавалер международных медалей и орденов, в т.ч. под эгидой ЮНЕСКО; звание "Золотое Перо Руси"; звание МАЭСТРО; звание МАСТЕР ПОЭЗИИ; звание ВЫДАЮЩИЙСЯ УЧЕНЫЙ ИЗ КОНСОРЦИУМА Международной Академии Этики в Индии. Внесена в Платиновую книгу СПСА за активные созидательные продвижения и большие успехи в творчестве и в связи с 20-летием Союза -НАВЕЧНО.

Ее Песни исполняются на радио «Радар», «Рецитал», «Феникс», «МЫ ВМЕСТЕ», АВТОРАДИО, Радио ОК, Радио НГ, Талант-Парк, Океан+, видео-проекте «Интрига-шоу». Участник ТВ передач на канале "Артист ТВ".

Every Child lifeline /DEMO GOG international magazine

СПСА—Натали Биссо

Понятие слова Счастье

Самый счастливый человек тот, кто даёт счастье наибольшему числу людей. (Д. Дидро)
Кому не дано вынести счастье и благополучие другого человека, тот сам счастлив никогда не будет! (Автор)

Вообще, сколько на земле индивидуумов, столько значений слова счастье, потому как каждый человек, в это понятие вкладывает свой смысл, подразумевает что-то особенное и своё.

Некоторым для счастья нужна самая малость, иногда умещающаяся в одном слове, другим - очень много, причем в основном, это - материальные блага, которые, по их мнению, и по их меркам всегда недостаточны и главное в жизни. Правильно! Бог сотворил человека для жизни на Земле, дал ему самосохранение и стремление к комфорту, но не значить, что это должно быть единственным и главным критерием и мерой счастья.

«Счастье – это когда тебя понимают». Понимание – это очень важный фактор человеческих отношений.

Человек должен бережно, с должным вниманием относится к проявлению чувств и отношения к нему. И это понимание состояния души любимого и дорогого тебе человека, просто человека, с которым ты имеешь дело – очень важно.

Я бы сказала, что - Счастье, когда в тебе нуждаются и ты кому-то нужен.

Наделенные Божественным даром люди, не нуждаются в пропаганде своих трудов, многие ученые отдавали науке все свое свободное время только для достижения поставленной цели и задач, и это было для них главным. Делали это не считаясь со своим временем, порой здоровьем и совершенно бескорыстно.
Лауреаты Нобелевской премии Мария и Пьер Кюри писали «Извлечение коммерческих выгод не соответствует духу Науки, идее свободного доступа к знаниям.»

Большинству людей непонятно, что иногда моральное удовлетворение от результатов деятельности, достижений важнее и весомее материальных наград какими непомерно большими они не казались.

Некоторые недовольны своей судьбой, ищут виновных в этом. Как хорошо сказал Кен Кейс, соавтор романа «Заглядывая вперед» (1926 г.): «У нас всегда есть достаточно для счастья, если мы получаем радость от того, что имеем и не тревожимся о том, чего у нас нет. И всему свое время, которое каждый представляет по разному».

По мнению выдающегося французского просветителя Жан Жака Руссо «Делать добро – это самое истинное Счастье, какое только может быть ведомо человеческому сердцу (душе)

Все мы явно или тайно мечтаем о счастье и радости, предпочитаем печалиться о том, что не сбылось, чего нет, сомневаемся в том, будет ли оно – счастье. Нельзя сидеть годами, сложа руки и дожидаться счастья. Его надо уметь заслужить. Учитесь, развивайтесь, сделайте добро кому-либо от чего он или она станут радостнее, счастливее и эта радость и счастье, которые вы подарили другому человеку вернется вам через призму Вселенной, усиленной.

Если разобраться, то окажется у нас очень много переживаний по пустякам и надуманным доводам без особых на то причин.
Живите реально и настоящим!

МАММАДОВА САРИЯ АГА МАММАД., Республика Азербайджан, кандидат наук, обладательница 140 научных трудов и двух авторских свидетельств, Член корреспондент МАНИ, академик МАРЛИ, Президент Международной Палаты Писателей и деятелей искуства ЦИЕСАРТ ИНТЕР КОНТИНЕНТАЛ от Республики Азербайджан, Почётный всемирный советник FOWCAAS «Федерации всемирного общества культуры и искусства (Сингапур). Обладательница более 50 дипломов разных стран Мира, в том числе как участник художественных конкурсов; большого числа Орденов и медалей. Редактор журнала"Общество и женщина". Является обладательницей "Золотого пера" СМИ Азербайджана «ЗОЛОТОГО ПЕРА РУСИ». Лауреат Московской, Пушкинской Премий. Финалист Международной Лондонской премии и финалист Международной Премии Мира. Кавалер ордена «Святой Анны», Медали Королевы Виктории, Петра Первого и др. Член Союза Писателей Азербайджана. Член Российского Союза Писателей (РСП) Полноправный Член Интернационального Союза Писателей. Член Союза писателей Северной Америки. Индивидуальный член Евразийской творческой Гильдии ЛОНДОН (ECG). Член Международной Литературной Ассоциации "Творческая Трибуна" (МЛАТТ).

Every Child lifeline /DEMO GOG international magazine
СПСА—Натали Биссо

Вселенная любви

Сказочна любви нашей вселенная.
У неё цветочное дыхание,
Память у любви в веках нетленная,
У любви – особенная мания.

У любви глубины океанные,
В них таятся яды наслаждения.
И к любви взывают неустанные
Переливы сладостного пения.

Трепетно, как ветра дуновение,
Рук, любимых нежное касание.
Бесконечна у любви вселенная
И слова любви, и миг молчания.

У любви святыми поцелуями
Жизнь, подобно радуге, расцвечена,
Растекается энергий струями
Благостное чувство человечное.

О любви останутся предания,
И картины выткут перламутрами,
О любви запишет Мироздание
Песни в облаках и строки мудрые.

© Раиса Мельникова, Вильнюс, Литва

Творческая биография

Раиса Мельникова – поэт, прозаик, публицист, переводчик. Живёт в Литве, в Вильнюсе. Автор 32 книг. Стихи и проза публиковались более чем в семидесяти альманахах разных стран мира, переводились на другие языки. Является членом международных писательских союзов, секретарём и вице-президентом МЛАТТ/ ILACT. Академик МАРЛИ. Лауреат девяти Международных конкурсов и фестивалей.

Every Child lifeline /DEMO GOG international magazine
Italian poetry page

UNTITLED

The night I look for air

Your music tastes like earth
from there you come

It stinks your memory
Mildew on your roots
Read in your stables
Wounded today by the snot

We are ticks in celebration
That do not come off
Yet.

UNTITLED

Be threshold.
Flat memory
And as a broken chipped statuette
Fragile. One piece missing.
Chocolate deception
Migraine is assured.
Be threshold.

Piece of the world
soundless.

UNTITLED

I want the heavy sheet to mark in
Black the end line.

Death at the end of the story
There is no discontinuous and
If you find him please continue with
Drawing. Remove the breaks.

A year of war generates fear
And havoc. Oppressed world.

Every Child lifeline /DEMO GOG international magazine

Italian poetry page

Serena Rossi
"I am"   SOLO SHOW
curated by Felice Terrabuio
Thursday 2 - Wednesday 22 November 2023
**Mimumo
MICROMUSEOMONZA
(visible 24/24h)
House of Luna Rossa(Sec. XIII) street Lambro 1 Monza
ITALY**
visible on Facebook
TITLE I We
Year 2023
Dimensions 220x140 cm
Acrylic on plastic

We are.
Within the one multitudes.
Memories are traces of lives lived
Indelible. The sounds the smells the loves
Condensed in body and mind in one
That is undone in many. These we are one.
And time is remembered.
Quiet shared space immemorial. It makes its way travelled
And passable. It exists inside and expands, exiting forever.
Imprinted as a tattoo from birth primordial star.
So we find ourselves in a simple primitive position without laying.
Without deception without any construction.
Alone and together
To the pride on display of ourselves. I am.

Serena Rossi November 2023

**I stamp on canvas a subject that is you
I am and
we are together without pose, without makeup without dress, soul only.
So I suspend time, freeze with the image even the instant out, thing that there is great need.
Time to reflect. Time to just be, to breathe, to think, to be there.
Just be there. Now.**

SERENA ROSSI

Visual Artist and Poet of Milan.

Serena Rossi was born in Milan in 1972. In 1999 she graduated in Pharmacy. She follows several courses in visual arts, since 2002 she exhibits his works in Italian and international exhibitions and some of them are part of collections private and public as the Open Air Museum of Camo and the Collection of the BPL. In 2011 she exhibits at the 54th Venice Biennale at the Italian Pavilion in Turin at the invitation of the critic Sgarbi.

In 2022 she participated in the call Rodello art and exhibited in the Church of the Immaculate of Rodello a large site specific work entitled Pray for us, which gives to the Museum of the Diocese of Alba, the exhibition collective International The sacred and the fragile from June to October 2022 curated by Enrica Asselle. In parallel since 2012 she deals with the same themes of poetry and publishes her syllogists and on different anthologies her poetry, last book published "Spaces" in Italian and Romanian ed. Cosmopoli edited by Eliza Macadan. She collaborates with several literary publications on the net and since 2022 she has been part of the Milanese editorial staff of the online cultural magazine Il pensiero mediterraneo and she founds the Literary and Artistic Competition Life the reality. In recent years she receives several awards and she merits reports to national literary competitions and international.

Every Child lifeline /DEMO GOG international magazine

Italian poetry page

Lidia Chiarelli is one of the Charter Members of **Immagine & Poesia**, the art literary Movement founded in Torino (Italy) in 2007 with Aeronwy Thomas.
Installation artist and collagist. Coordinator of #DylanDay in Italy.
She has become an award-winning poet since 2011 and she was awarded a Certificate of Appreciation from The First International Poetry Festival of Swansea (U.K.) for her broadside poetry and art contribution. Awarded with the Literary Arts Medal – New York 2020.
Six **Pushcart Prize (USA)** nominations. Grand Jury Prize at **Sahitto International Award 2021**.
In 2014 she started an inter-cultural project with Canadian writer and editor Huguette Bertrand publishing E Books of Poetry and Art online. Poetry Star, China 2022. Winner of KEL 2022.
Her writing has been translated into 30 languages and published in more than 150 Poetry magazines, and on web-sites in many countries.

https://lidiachiarelli.jimdofree.com/

https://lidiachiarelliart.jimdofree.com/

https://immaginepoesia.jimdofree.com/

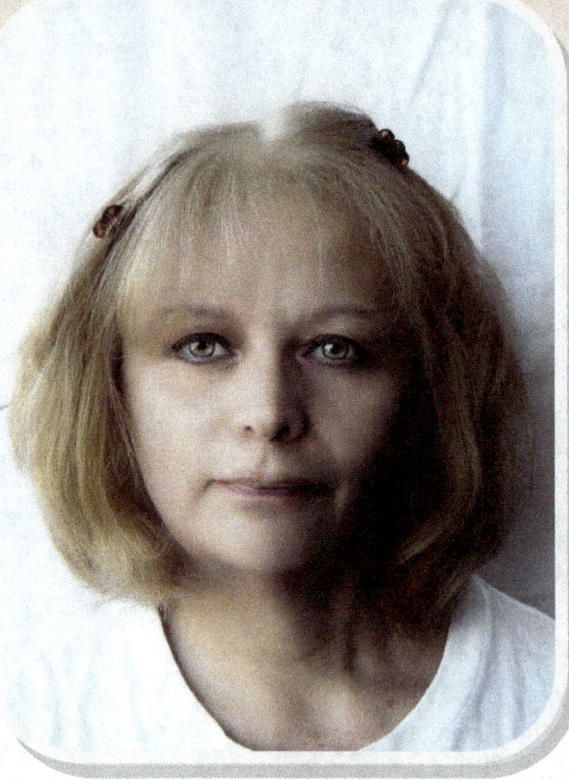

Every Child lifeline /DEMO GOG international magazine

Italian poetry page

Image & Poetry

for Jackson Pollock

Pollock-Krasner House, East Hampton

Now at last
I see you
Jackson Pollock
kneeling on the floor
handling sticks and brushes
dripping paints on your canvas.

From the dark night of your mind
a different universe emerges

new galaxies
(long looping lines)
take form

as your hands move rapidly around

formless and timeless realms
where I sink deep and deeper
wrapped in the colours
of your Greyed Rainbow.

For a while I will linger and listen to
the silence of the ocean

(or maybe to the roaring motor of your Oldsmobile convertible)

then – tonight –
I will write a poem just for you

Parables of Light

(to my father Guido Chiarelli*, pioneer for the lighting projects in Torino)

I love looking at the clouds in flight
slipping into the shadows of memories
seeing again those moments that lasted for years
when life had just begun
and
the evening sky revealed only for us
unreal colors.

In our summer walks
the streetlamps would light up suddenly
as if by magic
and competing with the moon and the stars
invented parables of light.

A cluster of distant images
that today recompose and break
in the blurred kaleidoscope of my mind.

*https://en.wikipedia.org/wiki/Guido_Chiarelli

LIDIA CHIARELLI, ITALY

Every Child lifeline / DEMO GOG international magazine

Portuguese poetry page

Isilda Nunes is a portuguese artist, writer and poet, Doctor Honoris Causa in Philosophy, Letters, Arts and Humanities in Barcelona. She won numerous awards and recognitions in many countries and she is part of the board of directors of several cultural movements both nationally and internationally and among other positions she is Founder of UMEA (Association of the World Union of Writers and Vice President of UMEA (World Union of Writers and Artists); Chairperson of the Language, Literature and Oratory Art Committee of Modern Pythian Games; Advisor to the Presidency of CIESART (International Chamber of Writers and Artists) and President of CIESART-Portugal; National Director of IFLAC World- Portugal; Vice-President MEL (Mulheres Empreendedoras da Lusofonia); Ambassador of the Women's Federation for Word Peace International; RRM3 Advisor for GPLT-UK- UN & EU, Ambassador for Peace and Humanity IFCH Morocco; Member of the Board of Directors of Editorial

Anger moves mountains
Faith melts glaciers
Hate shortens distances
The path to infinity is born and ends in us
Stairs are built to go up to hell
We let ourselves slip by falling
Descending to the cellars of heaven
While we wait
We feed this purgatory alive
In which we die in slow fire
Drowned in frozen sorrows
That burn feelings like firewood
Where ideas shuffle like cards
Writing new meaningless verses
On pages of life still to be lived
And us?
We sail aimlessly
Why?
Because with destiny
We would get there faster

WHERE DOES THE ANNOUNCED SPRING HOVER?

without a future,
chimeras wander
on the dying Earth.
insanity determines the direction.
no dove of peace can cross the darkness
nor the shadows of ignorance.
only pain,
lament and prayer.
in the room of rescue,
where the spectres reside
Hope agonizes.
the naive sleep of childhood threatened.
Chronos charts the course.
the old, from the uninhabited embrace
pray to escape
the crematory flow.
on the dying Earth,
some are just cemeteries.
And me?
And you?
And the announced spring?

Álvaro Maio is a portuguese periodist, writter, poet and singer, Doctor Honoris Causa in Philosophy, Letters, Arts and Humanities in Barcelona.
He has received several awards both at national and international level and he is President of UMEA (Association of the World Union of Writers) and International Director of the CIESART Cycle of Conferences 2023

Every Child lifeline / DEMO GOG international magazine

Alberto Pereira, Portuguese writer. Born in Lisbon. He is a member of PEN Portuguese Club. He has published eleven books. He was awarded the following literary prizes: 1 st place in the Poetry Contest Agostinho Gomes (2013); 1 st place in the Literary Contest Manuel António Pina (2013); Honorable Mention in the International Poetry Prize Glória de Sant' Anna (2018 and 2020); Honorable Mention in the International Poetry Prize Natália Correia (2021); Cesar Vallejo International Prize – Literary Excellence (2021); Ulysses Literary Prize (2023).

Lusitanian poets

The best answer to today's derogatory times
Resides in the persistent who write in verse
Eternal lanterns that erase oblivion
Poets looking for the reckless and pointless comma
Preventing it from reigning in the world
Walking along the sphinx itineraries to discover
Frowning in surprise the faces of lucidity
And advancing without fear or pity
In search of redemption, they cheat death by writing
Wrapped in the blood that slides down the pen

Alexandre Faria was born in Luanda, Angola, is a lawyer and a writer, and lives in Cascais, Portugal. He holds a degree in Law from the Faculty of Law of the University of Lisbon and has two Magna Cum Laude PhD's in Sports Management and in Sociology.
In 2012 he was awarded the 1st Degree Diploma from the Government of the Republic of Moldova. The following year, he received the Ulysses Grant International Prize from the City of Bolama and the Order of Honor from the Republic of Moldova, the highest civilian distinction in the country. In 2016 he received the Estoril Praia Merit Award and in 2017 he was distinguished with the Medal of Honor of the Parish of Alcabideche. In 2021, he was awarded with the Diploma of Merit of the City of Bolama, by the Ministry of Territorial Administration and Local Power of the Republic of Guinea-Bissau, as well as the Diploma of Merit of the Secretary of State for Culture of the Republic of Guinea-Bissau, for his cultural and literary path. In 2022, his novel "Magic Village" was awarded the Júlio César Andrino Literature Award - Best Work.
Lecturer in Portugal and abroad, he is the author of the three novels, four essays, one youth book and three poetry books.

I

The poems did not like my neighbourhood.
Misery was a skyscraper,
so, when they asked me
where I lived,
I would say,
New York.

There were men with wine in the place of blood.
Women smelled of an eternal wake,
children said things
unknown to postmen.

"Politicians are letters without a postcode".

Economists, they spent time
swapping the coins we had at home for emptiness.

My parents hated mail,
it brought invites to the court.
Then police officers would come and handcuff the house.

We would leave.

There was not a roof anymore,
walls would remain without screams
and the saints could take a peek at our heritage.

I would ask,
how does one shut the doors to the acid?

My father looked like a hospital,
he had afflictions.
There was mustiness in his eyes.
I, with the fingers
would draw a large idea,
would hold their dust.

I did not understand,
if there are four seasons
why was it always Autumn in my mother.
In her everything fell.
The days had been,
walls that were mistaken for birds,
clouds interpreted as wings,
pollen for the depressed beehive.
When tears overflew,
her face would turn into a river
and I,
would leave her kisses for boats.

Time put me in the shipwreck.
I did not control the reins on the wind
and as Sylvia Plath rightly said,
"the voice of God is full of draftiness".

Now I know,
Autumn is an identity card,
it legally speaks about many bodies.

Every Child lifeline /DEMO GOG international magazine

Portuguese poetry page

Jorge Castelo Branco was born in Porto, Portugal on November 20, 1965. Lives in Viseu. He is a translator and editor (Edium Editores - Porto, 2003/2012, Temas Originais – Coimbra 2010-2012); he is, currently, the editor of Seda Publicações (Matosinhos, since 2012) and Gugol Livreiros (Viseu, since 2018).

YOU LEFT IN ME

You left in me
The veil of a poem
The strength of your embrace
The touch, delicate and tender
The gaze, sweet and profound.

You left in me
The misted shroud of silence
The timid gestures, unsure
The warm whispers
Desire unbound.

You left in me
The might of the wind
The birds' flight
The cradle of waves
The semblance of the sea.

You left in me
The written page
A nascent romance's trace
In an empty car
Filled with ourselves.

Aida Araújo Duarte

THE ARCHANGEL OF SILENCE

In the silence of all things
I find the polyphony of everything.

And in the chords there are color, shape
The noise of silence.

In the silence of all things
I find the serenity of everything.

And in the colors there is music, sound
On the blank palette.

AIDA ARAÚJO DUARTE, a Portuguese writer and poet, has a degree in Romance Philology from the University of Coimbra. She has published the following works: " Daughter of the Mountain and the Wind and other stories of affection" (short story); " Absent Limpidity" (poetry); Lucinda's Sandals (novel), "VILLA DE BASTO"; "Dreams fly from the battlements" (novel). She wrote for the theatre: "Pancada da Vida" and "A Zulmira Abespinhada ". She translated: "Les Roses" by Rainer Maria Rilke and "Terre des Hommes" by Antoine de Saint-Éxupéry.

Every Child lifeline /DEMO GOG international magazine

Portuguese poetry page

I do not care about anything else
A certain Portuguese melancholy
Run off windows and embraced
Like one lost and dizzy bird
The streets of Serpa Pinto and Capelo Ivens.
All towns and cities have their arms coat
Of shattered drums and longing malaria`s
that goes from Street Serpa Pinto to Capelo Ivens.
Refuge I take from the mineral flavor,
Of the sturdy pavement and the rough clod
Of the coffee with gauzy sensuality
Like my mortal desperation.
Each flint of Serpa and Ivens
It is a step of thistles down to hell.
The beauty after all will not win .
Looking deeper the stomach always wins.
Let alone this strange blue and his mysterious work;
A philosophy of hatches in neon boulevards
Worth more than one centimeter in life won?
Besides us there is death or we can call it
Serpa Pinto and Capelo Ivens streets. (Now comes to mind broken pots, rags, and old books mouse bited by time).
Let me set it, an be less emphatic; embrace me slowly and without return, because I do not care about
anything more.

Olga Sotto is a Portuguese artist, writer, poet and investigator. She has a PhD in Education, a post-graduate degree in Clinical Gerontology and has various training courses in theatre and music. She has participated in theatre and television productions. She is the founder of the Education, Art and Heritage Project - EAP. She is the author of several books of poetry and poetic-musical projects and the author of the books on Art and Heritage Education: Education, Art and Heritage I; Convent of Christ, Education, Art and Heritage II; National Pantheon, Education, Art and Heritage III; Mafra National Palace, Education, Art and Heritage IV; Batalha Monastery (published by the Directorate-General for Cultural Heritage - DGPC).

State of the soul in democracy

**Faced with the advancement of inequality and social indifference,
There are entire communities of high egos,
Shocking scenarios worldwide,
False modesty and exacerbated pride,
State of emergency and democracy,
What difference does the strong restriction make now?...
If you never authorized me in your "sovereignty" ...
Has it never affected my rights to life in communion?
Have I always had freedom of expression and information?
What about my personal identity and citizenship rights?
Freedom taken by two rumors,
You lift a flower and who would have thought,
That in a move doesn't even lift your uprights
Two unequal worlds do not touch by color,
They don't wave out of love, they don't love out of spite...**

Paulo Seara is a Portuguese writer and poet with a degree in Animation and Artistic Production Practitioner.
Published work:
ACrónicas do Demencial - O porquê do Síndrome NilhooA (2007)
"Livro Daninho" (2016) Edições Bicho de Sete Cabeças;
"Take Away" (2017) Edições Bicho de Sete Cabeças;
"Spaghetti with Oil and Salt" (2020) Author's Edition;
"Motorway" (2021) Out of print.

Every Child lifeline / DEMO GOG international magazine

Anila Bukhari ASIA

Every Child lifeline /DEMO GOG international magazine

Face of the continent

Anila Bukhari, a remarkable individual from Pakistan, is a true force of inspiration. With her unwavering dedication, she has become a beacon of hope for children's rights, women's empowerment, and peace. Anila's poetic prowess has touched the hearts of readers in over 50 countries, transcending language barriers and spreading love and positivity. Her journey as a writer began at a young age, and she has since used her talent to make a difference in the lives of orphaned children through her project "Hopeful Hugs." By providing dolls and spreading love, Anila has brought smiles to the faces of countless homeless children, reminding them that they are not alone. Anila's passion for education and equality shines through her advocacy for girls' education. She believes that every child, regardless of their background, deserves access to quality education. Her dedication to this cause has earned her recognition and numerous awards, including the International Community Service Award and the International Book Peace Award. Through her poetry, Anila has created a platform for self-expression and empowerment. Her words have adorned the walls of art galleries, community centers, and cafes, captivating audiences and inspiring change. Her ability to capture the essence of human emotions and experiences is truly remarkable. Anila Bukhari is a shining example of how one person can make a profound impact on the world. Her dedication to helping others, promoting peace, and spreading love through her poetry is an inspiration to us all. With her words, she continues to touch lives and create a brighter future for generations to come.

Hyperpoem a ray of Hope

In the realm of friendship, we are blessed,
Like flowers, our words bloom, no gender oppressed.
With hearts united, we shine so bright,
In the hyper poem's embrace, we find our might.

No barriers of religion or creed,
Just pure connection, fulfilling our need.
Our friendship knows no bounds or divide,
In this beautiful language, we confide.

With poetic grace, our words align,
Creating a tapestry, so divine.
In unity, we stand tall and strong,
Together, we triumph, where we belong.

Let the hyper poem be our guide,
As we journey together, side by side.
In this language, we find our voice,
In friendship's embrace, we rejoice.

So let us continue to write and share,
Spreading love and kindness, showing we care.
Our grammar may vary, but our hearts are true,
In this hyper poem, our friendship shines through.

Every Child lifeline /DEMO GOG international magazine

Vietnamese Poetry Page

Author: Tran Thi Viet Trung
Born in 1956
Living and working in Thai Nguyen city (Thai Nguyen province)
Member of Literature and Arts Association of Vietnamese Ethnic Minorities
Member of Vietnam Writers' Association

Literature works published:
5 poetry collections
9 books on literature research and criticism
Awards
Many National and Local Literature Awards!

Changing the color of clouds
By Tran Thi Viet Trung

I can make your soul green
When the winter color starts to change the season on that age.
But how cruel and pitiful,
When I can't make your white hair - turning black!

I'm so late – therefore I'm so fragile
Can't stop the life flow like a waterfall.
Dear white clouds - Please change for you!
This black hair - Let be the same white!

Dear! Let be...
By Nong Thi Ngoc Hoa

I have a head scarf
It is likely a little sun
I have a green belt
It is silky as the color of corn and rice

The sun gives me a fire
For never being cold
The belt rolls around my small waist
It is passionate even in a dream

Even crossing three passes and seven mountains
Even crossing nine streams and ten villages
Dear! Let be the scarf
Dear! Let be the belt.

Poet: Nong Thi Ngoc Hoa
Born on December 2, 1955
Hometown: Yen Thinh - Cho Don - Bac Kan
Resident: Tan Dan, Viet Tri, Phu Tho
Member of Literature and Arts Association of Vietnamese Ethnic Minorities;
Member of Vietnam Writers' Association;

Published 12 poetry and epic collections
Received many Central and Local Literary Awards

Every Child lifeline /DEMO GOG international magazine
Vietnamese Poetry Page

Poet Mac Khai Tuan

Date of birth: October 15, 1955
Homeland: Ninh Binh
Member of Literature and Arts Association of Vietnamese Ethnic Minorities
Many published literature works including memoirs and poetry collections.

White tears
Poet Tran Thai Hong

The women who have not had time to smile fully
in the deviated world, hands holding flowers must firmly hold the guns
petals of roses faded in the broken afternoon*
deeply sad sunset tinged with mourning color

Inclining the head to the war loss
lighting incense sticks for the persons who laid down
every battlefield is painful for those who stay
all mothers would cry when they lose their children

Whispering
Poet Mac Khai Tuan

When you sit enjoying the sunshine of the day
Please stop be angry to express the night story
When you stand watching the moon rise
Please stop blame the wind forgetting the sad sound
When you feel a little sadness

Please stop be indifferent, the dew drops at the temple door
When the heart is pity with swinging wings
Please come back to the garden with sparse leaves
To see people writing the wise verses
Please play the sad songs... and go

Poet Tran Thai Hong
Born in February 09, 1960
Resident: My An commune, Mang Thit district, Vinh Long province
Head of branch, Vietnam Writers' Association in Vinh Long province

Literature works published:
4 poetry collections and 1 to be published soon

Literature prize:
* Prize C (no prize A) for the poetry collection "Day of dream"
*Consolation Prize for poetry collection "Behind the wind"
*Consolation Prize for poetry collection "Desert of the day"
*And some other prizes.

Every Child lifeline / DEMO GOG international magazine

Vietnamese Prose Page

Poet: Dinh Thi Thuy Hang
Born: April 15, 1963
Hometown: Binh Luc - Ha Nam
Member of Literature and Arts Association of Vietnamese Ethnic Minorities
Member of Literature and Arts Association of Yen Bai Province

Literature works published:
A poetry collection "There is such place waiting for you"
Many articles published in central and local newspapers and magazines

The reverting place
Poet: Dinh Thi Thuy Hang

The reverting place where its spiritual energy is eternal
Full of scarlet, the infatuated love
Suddenly, so peaceful listening to thousands of falling petals
Lightly, relaxedly - I'm back to the motherland

Waves of spreading water, it hugs me gently
Weaving magically for the last time to welcome the dawn
The wind is gentle and the birds are chirping
Sun drops are clear, bees are looking for honey

Simple wooden roofs, the silent moss
This is the reverting place where it settles the soul
Stepping lightly, listening to the stone road to name:
Cinnamon forest, Pine forest, Cunninghamia lanceolata, Brunfelsia Hopeana...

Returning to the ancient times - the origin of the nation
The houses carry homeland identities
Nestling below the Hmong's peach forest and stone houses
Floating in the harmony nature

I return to my childhood catching butterflies
Back to the Origin so that the soul to be reverted

Chrysanthemums and birdsong
Poet Truc Linh Lan

I drifted along with a long dream
Lost in foggy memories
The puppets were dancing on the stage
Fake flowers decorated too much beauty
I saw the faith hidden in secret corners
The echoed sound was illusive
Drifting away in ephemeral singing
Drifting away... frivolous literary pages
Drifting away the screaming verses

On the table
Bunches of chrysanthemums
A wine glass is very purple
I gather the time to get a smile
A wind pushes sadness and joy through each season of falling leaves
I will dream that I would be cold by heavy rain
The clock on the wall would be stopped before and after
A little book opens narrow pages of life
I ignite in the ashes of the kitchen corner thin smoke cluster.

Outside
The sound of singing birds in the sky lightly
Small door frame
An ashoka flower has just bloomed.

Poet Truc Linh Lan
Born in 1953 in Can Tho.
Member of Literature and Arts Association of Vietnamese Ethnic Minorities
Member of Vietnam Writers' Association;
Published works: 2 sets of novels; 3 poetry collections; 2 critical and reasoning volumes

Every Child lifeline /DEMO GOG international magazine

Vietnamese Prose Page

Poet Nguyen Thanh Binh
Date of birth: December 26, 1953
Hometown: Nam Trang, Truc Noi, Truc Ninh, Nam Dinh
Formal University Lecturer
Member of Literature and Arts Association of Vietnamese Ethnic Minorities
Member of Literature and Arts Association of Phu Tho
Member of Vietnam Journalists' Association
5 poetry collections published so far

Sediment words on Tan Vien Mountain
Poet/Musician/Artist Bang Ai Tho

Tonight, on the green forest
A little song flies over the wind
The old stories whisper beside the grass
Joining the streams to sing thousands of songs

It's raining late tonight in Vien Son mountain
A raining proposal, the blurred moon on 16th lunar day
Tonight, I come out of the sadness so lovely
Amidst the deep night to be a motionless human
         Quietly washing the forest rain

Waiting for the dawn
         People take people to the mountain
Listen to the wind offering the sediment words
Beside the nine-tusk elephant
Nine-cockspur chicken, nine-pinkfeather horse*

Tonight a star is as cold as a drop of glass
Touching the flickered wind...
Flickering... to listen to the rain singing my fate!

* Rare animals only in Vietnamese fairy tales

It belonged to
Poet Nguyen Thanh Binh

It belonged to me
Childhoods
Not just dreams
It belonged to me
Teenage years
Not just went to school
It belonged to me
Homeland
Not just sweet fruits
It belonged to me
A promise...
Not said a goodbye
You got married
The bitter fruit belonged to me...

It belonged to me grandmother's praying
Continuity
Sadness
Hardship
All along since was the student
I remember
All along for whole Lifetime
Hopely still remember...

Whole lifetime is busy with books
I don't know much
Another world
Belongs to...

Poet/Musician/Artist Bang Ai Tho
Born on August 30, 1958 in Hanoi
Member of Literature and Arts Association of Vietnamese Ethnic Minorities
Member of Vietnam Writers' Association;
There are many literature works published in the country and in the world.
Many literature and arts awards

Every Child lifeline /DEMO GOG international magazine
Vietnamese Poetry Page

Poet Do Thi Tac
Born: July 23, 1963
Homeland: Sy Quy village, Nguyen Hoa commune, Phu Cu district, Hung Yen province
Chairwoman of the Arts Literature Council, Arts – Literature Association of Lai Chau province
Head of Branch; Literature and Arts Association of Vietnamese Ethnic Minorities of Lai Chau province
Head of Branch; Association of Vietnamese Folklorists of Lai Chau province
Member of Literature and Arts Association of Vietnamese Ethnic Minorities
Member of Vietnam Writers' Association
Member of Association of Vietnamese Folklorists

Mountain mothers
Poet Do Thi Tac

Carrying seeds on their backs.
Carrying babies in front of their chests.
Passing through three forests.
Mothers walk uphill.
The sun is not awake yet.
The seeds sow into the soil.
The babies sleep well in the shack.
After sowing the seeds, lulling the babies, the mothers sing.
Begging for rain, the seeds will germinate.
May the soil proliferate many living seeds.
To raise children to be village boys and Muong girls.
Harvest reasons
To carry the living seeds on their backs.
To take babies in front of their chests.
Mothers heads are sun, rain, thunder, lightning
Passing through three forests
Returning to the village with the moon.
Mountain mothers
What to ask for themselves!

The night and I
Poet: Cao Thi Hong

Falling in the night
floating with many thoughts
white thoughts – white speckledness
red thoughts - red flicker
black thoughts – black zigzag...
pink browns, yellow purple...
                    vertically and horizontally running
tearing apart the night...

The rain yarns crisscross
the wind cuts the broken space
floating in the night
I look at myself silently...

Desiring a sincere word from God
thirsty to drink Lover's warm lips...
wishing that the age could be rejuvenated...
don't rush to wonder at the galaxy...

 deep in the night...deep in the color of thoughts...
the silk threads entangle in the way to return...
I cry alone for myself
as if
  I got lost in the night...
  the night lost in me...

Poet: Cao Thi Hong
Born in 1968
Hometown: Sam Son, Thanh Hoa
Member of Literature and Arts Association of Vietnamese Ethnic Minorities;
Member of Vietnam Writers' Association;
Member of Culture and Arts Association of Thai Nguyen Province

Main literature works: 7 published literature works, including poetry collections; critical theory books; critical research books and others

Every Child lifeline /DEMO GOG international magazine

Vietnamese Poetry Page

Poet Bui Viet Phuong
Born: March 25, 1980
Vice President of Literature and Arts Association of Hoa Binh Province
Member of Literature and Arts Association of Vietnamese Ethnic Minorities
Member of Vietnam Writers's Association
Member of Vietnam Journalists' Association

Literature works published:
- 2 poetry collections
- 1 critical essay collection
- 4 prose collections

Awards: C Prize, Vietnam Union of Literary and Art Associations, C Prize, Military Arts Magazine And many other awards...

The rebirth
Poet Ngo Thanh Van

Movingmyself
struggling in a tight shirt
in a chaos thought
words found me

seeing me asleep on the hill
dreaming of the far away horizon
thousands of twinkling stars
on the river with crashing waves

I sing a song for myself
autumn short passage. And old things
old thoughts
old words
old ideas
the train runs on the old rail
lulling me

in heaven dreams
seeing me to fly towards the sun
tearing the cover off
burning body into the fire
burning myself
Rebirth.

Our village
Poet Bui Viet Phuong

Just asking for three hundred trees for wood from the forest
Then take back the blade
The village in the middle of the forest that everything is enough
Greed has roots, but no one digs

The village is not lack of elderly people in many years
Children some dislike, some stay in
Growing up to love each other, not found an excuse yet
My family had to accept the groom far away
The village has more people but the heart is like weevilled wood
Going back and forth, the thorns are no longer sharp
Companying together to the streams and fields
Two guys drink together
Walking unsteadily in the same way

During the war years, bombs fell, guns exploded
Hundred years the village reserved the boys
Like a forest that has been harvested wood for thousands of years
To the battlefield
Even if falling, it must be intact with wood grain
Even if don't know its names, the enemy must be afraid of
The village is with thirty roofs
Living with big trees, thinking deeply

Then the people exist, the rivers exist, the mountains exist
Still thirty roofs built from three hundred wood trees
Keeping to sow seeds, picking teas, leading buffaloes to the mountains
Our village, the dialect
Our village, clothes and scarfs
Never asked ourselves
Why does favourable weather in so many years

Poet Ngo Thanh Van
Born on June 12 in Gia Lai; Hometown: Nghe An.
Member of the Association of Literature and Arts of Vietnamese Ethnic Minorities;
Member of Vietnam Writers' Association;
Member of Gia Lai Culture and Arts Association.
Literature works published:
Through the memory region (Poetry collection); Whisper to You (A Collection of Short Stories); June 12 (Poetry); Night Sketch (Poetry); Listening to the breath of leaves (Poetry); Foreign land (A collection of short stories); Mist region and Streets (prose)
Awards:
- Young Prize of the Vietnamese Arts and Culture Association; Prize C of Gia Lai Provincial Arts and Culture Association; Fourth Prize, Xu Thanh Magazine; Consolation prizes of Gia Lai Provincial Culture and Arts Association; Prize C of Gia Lai Provincial Culture and Arts Award.

Every Child lifeline /DEMO GOG international magazine

Vietnamese Prose Page

On the Reed Hill

Short story by Vu Thao Ngoc

Winter of that year started to get cold. If wasn't busy with taking the children to evacuate, participating to dig fortifications of the town, Thuy's female colleagues in factory would also rush into knitting shirts and scarves for the children wearing in Lunar New Year. Yet, everything reversed. Hotter, more stressful, worrisome about the lives of the whole family had never been more tense than the strings...

That hill was the highest in the town, reeds, downy myrtle bushes grow densely during the Lunar New Year seasons. Reeds competed to bloom so the whole hill looks only white color. The white color of the hill gradually became the name of the townspeople - the Reed Hill. These days, the US raided the North of Vietnam more intense. Bombs dropped into the sea and residential areas devastating the whole town.

Families must send their children to the countryside for evacuation. Fortifications along the streets had been extended. Classes in the tunnels, straw hats loomed on the ways to classes under the fortification tunnels. The whole town was without electricity. People always tried to pay attention to the town siren to avoid bombs...

Thuy still remembered everything in that night. Ha returned at midnight. The first sentence when he saw his wife, Ha said that he was dispatched urgently. Thuy thought that it was midnight, he might stay until tomorrow morning. Ha still wore the same clothes that were covered with dust. He said as whispering "you stay at home and take care of mother and children, this time it's too urgent, leadership sends me urgently to study in the military zone, it seems like there is going to deal with a big fight. Try, don't be sad".

After that, Ha hugged Thuy and inhaled each other's scent, then he collected a few simple things and put them in the old faded backpack. Thuy remembered the parting night as seemed not parting. Thuy's emotion was always overflowed with private feeling between husband and wife. Ha stayed on the reed hill. Although it was only about half an hour walk from her house, but the spirit of battle was very tense, Ha must stick to the battlefield. He was assigned to be the captain of the artillery company. All week he must follow the battlefield. It was difficult to go down the mountain and look at the house for a while and then go in a hurry.

Military news was getting hotter every day, the ferry crossing the Bang River was still busy back and forth every day. That was the arterial road from the delta to the northern border, which was the key point that the US chose to attack and target. The US wanted to cut off all communication between the internal and external regions, and isolate all aspects among localities in the North. Therefore, the whole town was in a situation of alarm level. Everybody and works seemed no place for sadness or thinking. Every shift from home to work, the body was full of coal dust, Thuy immediately rushed in houseworks cooking for the mother-in-law and children. Her mother-in-law was old and weak, yet she had to hold granddaughter Tu all day long so that Thuy and Ha commited in the work of the factory and the battlefield.

Thuy gave birth to four children not far from each other. The children were like a flock of chicks living in a low wet house roof that supplied by the factory. The mosquito net stuck on the bad year-round could not be removed because every time the grandmother lulled Tu to sleep, the two younger children huddled together. Afraid of mosquitoes, she did not remove it. Thuy was too busy with a ton of works at the factory to care her four small children.

But in the afternoon, when Ha was not on duty, she could still breathe, but from the time she was on duty, Ha was completely on Reed Hill, leaving only Thuy to deal with that unnamed mountain of work. Rarely, Ha takes the opportunity to go home to ask her mother a question, encourage her wife, eat a bowl of rice quickly, and then finally go to Reed Hill. Ha said, the situation is still very tense, yesterday we were almost destroyed because of our target, fortunately the "thunder god, ghost" guy ignored it.

Ha was busy on duty on Reed Hill,

Writer Vu Thao Ngoc
The author who has won many specialized literature awards. She is especially successful in the field of literature on the topic of workers and women with a soft voice, rich in emotions and literature images. During her writing career so far, she published 27 literature works including novels, poetry collections, short stories, critical essays and literature works for children. Among them, the most impressive works are "Sun Valley" - a collection of short stories, "Moss and Stone" - a collection of poems, "Three Men" - a novel, "The furnace light" - a novel, and several other literature works.

Thuy managed to deal with that unnamed mountain of works. Rarely, Ha took the opportunity to go home visiting his mother, encouraging his wife, eating h a bowl of rice quickly, and then finally rush to the Reed Hill. His superiors said "the situation is still getting tense, the US seems to bring the North back to the stone age, it will bomb more, destroy the coal town…."

Every Child lifeline /DEMO GOG international magazine

Vietnamese Prose Page

"Oh, oh, I'm begging you, stop talking, don't leave me and mom at home worrying. You can be assured to go to the battlefield, I will take care of everything at home". After saying that Thuy prepared a handful of rice, wrapped the whole package of delicious pounded meat that she had just finished making.

Seeing that his wife packed the whole pounded meat to put it in his pocket, Ha tried to smile and said, "Dear, I won't take it, our daughter Tu is not well, let her eat. I will bring sesame seeds". Thuy had tears in her eyes, but her voice was resolute "no, you must bring it, this whole week, none of the soldiers have been able to come home, therefore, bring for them to eat with you".

Tomorrow to have a new month meat voucher, I will buy an advance for the next month quantity and then make more pounded meat for the children and mother, you can be assured.

That's it, you say goodbye to mother and go up the Reed Hill on duty. Don't make use of the commander to come home for a long time, if anything happens..."

"No, no, be assured"

"But today I also find it strange, every time the "gods of thunder and ghosts" humming like cicadas somewhere, today seems to be quiet. A bit strange, right?"

"That's correct. So I go. Mom, I'm going up the Hill to fight, don't worry. I'm sure the bad guy will only disturb for a few days, mom. My superiors also said that it is going to sign an agreement with the US in France, peace would be returned". Then he turned to his wife "Kiss the children for me" then Ha nudged Thuy slightly. She tried to smile and told Ha "You only got the joke".

Ha put on the old faded backpack and walked out of the alley. The mid-month moon has just risen to the top. Thuy heard as far as the rumbling sound of thunder gods, ghosts... That sound had been compressed into everyone's ears since the US dropped bombs to destroy the dormitory complex of the factory. It was far away the rumbling sound...

The moon night of the winter was clearer, Thuy can't sleep after the hard works from early morning for the whole family, especially just seeing Ha off. Thuy looked up at the Reed Hill. The moon scattered everywhere. The coal train crossed, the dormitory was as if dyed by the moonlight shining with coals... That night the siren was quiet, but the coal train stopped running because it seemed that an order temporarily not carrying coals to the ship in the port side.

It was colder at night.

The moon was also brighter.

The rumbling sound became clearer, at first it sounded far away, then closer, then roared quickly. The sand and soil suddenly turned upside down. The electricity of whole town was immediately turned off. Thuy's ears could no longer hear anything. All grandmother and the children hugged each other and rolled under the old bed. The ear-piercing sound was stopped after a long time, then it became strangely quiet. Someone shouted at the top of the dormitory.

"Brothers, our artillery company on the hill shot down the American plane, hurry over to Bai Chay ferry to see if the pilot is caught. This victory is just to celebrate, Ha - the commander of the self-defense company, will be awarded the title of hero this time. Let's celebrate, Mother Thuy, let's celebrate, Thuy..."

Thuy was almost in a panic, the tearing sounds made Thuy unable to distinguish between quiet and moving. When it was finally complete, the sky was just as bright. The first person from the artillery company on the Reed Hill came to inform Thuy that was Mr. Sang. When he saw Thuy, Sang said:

- Follow me. Tell grandma to take care of the kids.
- What's wrong, my husband...
- Follow me to the hospital
- Oh my god, my husband... my husband...
- No, I told you to follow me quickly, hurry up.

When Sang and she jogged to the provincial hospital, Thuy almost had no breath to walk, her husband's teammate had to support her but her legs kept so weak. She couldnot cry. She couldn't speak... Ha had sacrificed. Someone's voice spoke in her ears "Ha and his company coordinated very well with the air defense forces in the town to destroy a "thunder god", it was very heroic..."

Thuy collapsed completely, a pain that could not scream, could not cry out loud. Ha seemed falling in deep sleep. The piece of gauze wrapped around his black hair still bleeding, but it appeared in front of Thuy's eyes was a wreath of fire. Then it appeared in Thuy's eyes a wreath of roses that Thuy once told Ha "When our house will be no longer poor, the children grow up, I will plant many roses so that we can enjoy to watch the flowers in the morning in free time"

"The dream of roses is here. Dear Ha, Dear my husband…. Why did you leave your old mother, leave your children, leave me without saying a word". Thuy only uttered a few words that hurt in her heart, the other sounds that no one could hear clearly that she must have said just to let Ha hear...

The pain from that winter more than forty years ago that has never been forgotten. Her children have got married, but every time remembered that time, her heart still is painful. Every winter, she climbs the Reed Hill to find Ha. Thuy could sit there all day talking with Ha, with white reeds, with the immense wind blowing from the Bang River. She looks down at the busy town with the appearance of a modern city but her heart couldn't stop thinking. Knowing that Ha has gone far, far away, but for Thuy, it is only his trip going somewhere. With Thuy, he is still beside her, with his children on the Reed Hill.

Every Child lifeline /DEMO GOG international magazine

Vietnamese Prose Page

Chrysanthemum camellia

Short story by
Bui Nhu Lan

A.

Early morning in spring, it is full of flying dew. The dew entwines in floating clouds and mountains. But I don't know if it's dew, cloud, or drizzle. Every pure white cluster plays around on high and low mountains and then wonders to the villages. It seems that in the gentle spring wind, the lightly scent of bloomed peach, plum and pear flowers and the ethereal taste of bloomed chrysanthemum camellia calling for the Lunar New Year.

Dear you, on the occasion of the Lunar New Year, layers of Chrysanthemum camellia, which the mountain people called the "yellow flower tea", after many months accumulated the essence of mountain air, forest land, sky, sunshine ... now it bursts the sweet color. The buds are shy among the eyes of dark green leaves, brilliantly blooming under the dew, calling the collectors, making me to miss you very much.

The space is yellowish joy, full of fragrance. There is a soft, gentle sound the spring wind carrying the lightly flying pollen. Oh look! From the endless ethereal and elegant yellow color, countless beautiful round deweyes perch on petals, joyfully welcome spring. Suddenly my soul is joyful, full of emotion, like the day I was overwhelmed by your hypnotic look.

Emotionally I remembered. In the spring morning of last year, next to the ancient yellow flower tea tree, in the endless pollen, among thousands of sparkling deweyes, I was the first time passionated, overwhelmed by your passionate kisses. I confused to be melted in your open arms, shining smile. You lifted me up, turned with the flying yellow flower color. Just like that, until the two of us laughed loud and rolled. You lifted me up and then gently drifted, immersed, wet ... among the dewed grass.

Nowadays, in my sweet soft subconsciousness, I'm still surprised hardly believing that I have the happy fate in love. My childhood was spent in the guilt of two words "without father". My birth certificate doesn't include my father's name on it. He is a mystery in my life.

A small blood-drop of mine, an orphaned child, was the fruit of adversity. I don't understand why my mother exchanged her honor to have me, and then got bad reputation for whole life? My mother has a pain in the heart that is hard to speak out that I have never dared to ask. I'm afraid to touch her pain...

I grew up in her sad lullaby. At night, in the place of high mountain, my mother hugged me without stopping a heavy sigh. I innocently rested my head on mother's tear-soaked arm and slept well. Mother's life is like a thin quiet crescent moon. I grew up with her calloused wound. Mother received the pain of a human life, endlessly hoped with a full and open life for me...

*
* *

B

Afternoon Eva. The pot of sticky rice cakes simmers on the fired three-legged stove. Mother put a food tray on the altar and burned incense. The mother's gentle, round white face is silent and thoughtful. Mother prays to the forest god, ancestors... but it seems that she confides. So strange! Mother's voice is soft, steady, waving in the non-stop fire. My stomach curls up. I nestle closely to mother in the fragrant spreading incense.

Mother gently takes my hands, warms it in her palms. Mother's eyes blinkers slightly, fills with tears, she says: "Dear Xuan, tomorrow the first day of the Lunar New Year, you will turn twenty-four, the girl who holds The Cat." I smile softly, rub my head on mother as I was a baby. Mother caresses my hair gently: "Xuan, don't blame me because you don't have a father. That day, I was foolish..."

I am silent by the memory of mother's vivid, sad movie. Mother's voice suddenly softenes, brings me back to the past.

... She walked towards the high mountain. Behind her was the vibrant city and noisy district town. She left behind the hustle and painful love. In front of her eyes, high and low mountains rode dew, wore clouds with thousands of forest trees under the bright yellow sunshine. She received the decision to teach at the highlands. She walked as if she were running away. She cannot let parents get a bad reputation. Her family was exemplary in the eyes of people. They were teachers. Her elder brother was talented, successful and he worked as a teaching assistant at Thai Nguyen University.

Nowadays, she buried feelings to the bottom of her soul. She tried to forget that man. Did the love and the ebullience of youth blind her eyes? No! In her deep mind, he was a warm, loving man. She did not understand, why did he change his feelings so quickly? Just two months ago, after a passionate kiss, he whispered: "At the end of this year, let's go to your home". Leaned her head into his strong chest, listened to his heartbeat, she was filled with hope.

However, the desire for wealth

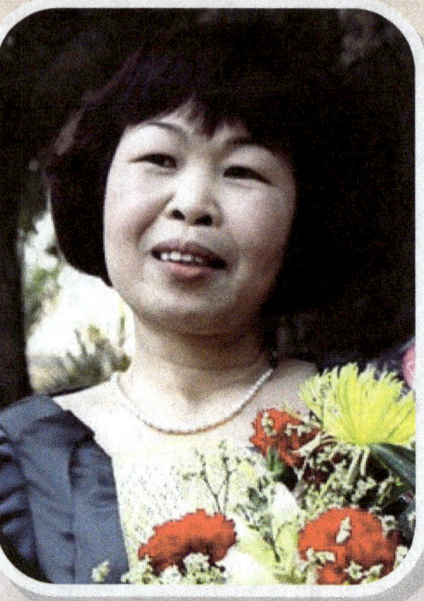

Writer Bui Nhu Lan
Year of birth: 1967; Ethnic: Tay
Address: Group 9, Thinh Dan ward, Thai Nguyen city

Member of Literature and Arts Association of Vietnamese Ethnic Minorities
Member of Literature and Art Association of Thai Nguyen Province
Member of Vietnam Writers' Association

12 literature works have been published so far and 14 different literature awards

pulled him away from her. He stepped into the flower car with the daughter of the real estate family. She was disappointed, painful, like someone holding a knife to cut her heart into a hundred pieces. However, she did not complain or blame. She quietly left, despite difficulties waiting ahead. In her belly there was a small drop of his blood and she was raising.

August. The autumnal cold breeze. She arrived at the Pu Nhi school. The school was in the middle of the village. Welcomed her at top of the slope was the Chief of A Chao village. In the sound of the strong wind, the Village Head said honestly:

Every Child lifeline /DEMO GOG international magazine

Vietnamese Prose Page

"Teacher, it's difficult up here, but the villagers like the teacher. Children expect the teacher's education a lot."

At night. Wrapped in a warm blanket but still cold. The mountain air and the cold breeze howled, released the cold into the empty little house. It was cold from her soul. The dew rolled on the leaves, the water under the ravine moaned and lamented... she was homesick, pitiful, bursted into tears, choking.

Pu Nhi school, all year round, covered by full of dew. The dew was so much that she felt as if she was floating among milky windy space. Every morning, she waited for the clearing dew, then started to teach. In winter, many days, pupils and teacher huddled in the cold dew, lit a fire to warm up, the dew flew away, the children could see the board clearly then they can start to learn words.

On morning of the first day of Lunar New Year, twenty-four years ago, Spring sunshine spreaded the sweet warmth. Her belly was round and tight, the day she was going to give a birth. She writhered, pursed her lips in pain as if someone was tearing her intestines. In the small house connecting the classrooms of the school site, the fragrance emitted from the pot of yellow flower tea, the village nurse, Ms. Say, encouraged: "Teacher, try hard, a baby is coming". Heaven and earth seemed to stop when a girl's cry "wa...oa...wa" resounded. She named her daughter as Xuan. Daughter had her last name Dao..."

Night. About half an hour left until heaven and earth will intersect, until the Eve. Mother told me that later, when I accidentally meet the man who gave me a shape and life, then will not be resentful. After all, I am still his blood drop.

Mother suddenly stops talking, stands up, quickly pickes up the sticky rice cakes. Gently, mother urges: "Daughter, call to wish your grandparents and the oldest family. Let's celebrate the Eve with the villagers" On mother's face is a bright, peaceful smile.

*   *   *
C
Pu Nhi villagers all year round live in the mountain, among the ancient yellow flower tea trees. Although knowing this species of forest tea, from its leaves to flowers, they are used as a very good drink. However, the villagers do not know that this is a rare and precious medicinal herb, called a "panacea".

I don't know how, mother propagates the benefits of Chrysanthemum camellia. Then the villagers listen the teacher going to the forest, up the mountain to pluck each yellow flower tea root, plant the hills around the village, creating a large tea forest. I and the children ran tired, still around a corner.

These kinds of tea are strange. Its purple-pink buds covered by the dew, washed by the wind, sunbathed to rise. The leaves turn dark green when the trees give sparkling yellow buds. Before Lunar New Year, some trees bloomed. When the spring breeze blows, sparkling flowers light up the sky.

Every year, after the second day of Lunar New Year, when worshiping the forest god, the villagers collect the flowers. On these days, many visitors from far away come to Pu Nhi. They come to travel, experience to pick and buy the Chrysanthemum camellia. Now, the Pu Nhi villagers live a well-off live from the yellow flower tea trees, combined with the "Homesday community tourism model".

Dear, I love its yellow color. I want to drop myself into the fragrant pollen, filled with the sound of flying bees. I like standing on the high mountains, looking at each house on stilts among dew, with thousands of bright Chrysanthemum camellia. The seasons of flowers cling to my feet, calling me back. I study at Thai Nguyen University of Agriculture and Forestry, wish to have a lot of scientific knowledge to develop Chrysanthemum camellia in the high mountains.

I remember very much, last year Lunar New year holiday, our class had a few months left before the university graduation exam, the whole class was eager to go to Pu Nhi to experience the "Homesday community tourism model". In the immense fragrance of tea, amidst the excitement to pick the yellow camellias, you whispered to me: "I will come here with you and the villagers, invest in producing products, and build a brand of the tea as foreign countries. Not sell fresh camellias any more"

At that time, even in the sweet yeast of love, I was suddenly afraid, one day your words would fly with the clouds and the blowing wind...

This Lunar New Year, the color of Chrysanthemum camellia is very beautiful, Pu Nhi village will be crowded with tourists because the covid epidemic has been controlled among the community. Yesterday afternoon you called me and whispered: "The Cat Lady of mine, I miss and love you very much. I have a secret for you!" And he bursted out laughing before the phone ended...

*   *   *
At morning of the first day of Lunar New Year, mother smiled cheerfully, asked "Our village welcomes tourists. Dear Xuan, will you be surprised when that person's family to talk for a hundred-year matter?". My ears seemed to have buzzle sound, my chest jumped strongly. What mother said was beyond my imagination! Very surprised, I suddenly whispered: "I love you, the street boy!"

At the moment, mother goes to visit the villagers and wish their good spring and drop the nice words at their houses. I am engrossed in watching the Chrysanthemum camellia forest to show its brilliance in the dizzle rain. Mother is not mine alone. Mother belongs to an ethnic group in Pu Nhi village.

Look! In the ethereal, immense and magical white dew region, the seductive yellow color of Chrysanthemum camellia, a group of cars driving uphill to the village. The soaring birds in the sky sing joyful songs welcoming the spring.

Every Child lifeline /DEMO GOG international magazine

Vietnamese Prose Page

The story father told at battlefields

short story by Doan Ngoc Minh

On summer nights, Tung's family often sits on the porch of the house on stilts. It is a floor made by bamboo stalks that used to dry rice, corn... On bright moon nights, parents, brother Lan and Tung enjoy the cool breeze blowing from the Hien river. Tung often lies on the stall with brother Lan counting the stars on the sky. But the most interesting thing is to listen father telling the thrilling stories when he fought in battlefields. Tonight, the same, father finishes a cup of forest tea, then he starts:

- Do you all want father telling the story on the battlefields?
- Yes...yes... father please tell us! We all respond joyful.

Mother brings a basket of hot boiled potatoes:

- The sweet potato is very sweet! She happily put the basket of sweet potatoes on the stall.

Father clears his throat again and slowly says:

The sun was already inclined on the far side of the Truong Son mountain range, the hot wind blowed in each wave sweeping the dust. When was in Laos, I felt how the Laos wind combining with the hot sun, the dry wind and sun made my arms peeling off in pieces, as if had not washed for a long time!

Lips were so dry, even though wearing a helmet, my head still felt as hot as fever. I felt that not only the sun, but the heat of the Laos wind was also the agent, blackening human skin! Suddenly a light move, I startled turning to the side of the tunnel wall:

A black snake, about the size of a wrist with an arm long, crawled out from the fallen trunks, along the tunnel wall. It was only half an arm's length away from me, it stopped and raised its head high right in front of my face. I sit like a statue, a moment later the snake lowered its head to the ground, slowly crawling inside the tunnel, perhaps it wanted to avoid the harsh sun here!

Three scout soldiers slept leaning against the wall, they had spent many nights awake to fight, so they were very tired. I slightly lowered my head to look at the snake, the light from the tunnel enough for me to see the snake slithering in and lying around, right next to the wood in the tunnel. "I should kill it to avoid biting the soldiers" I thought quickly. "Let's just ignore it, as long as the soldiers don't know there are snakes...". I reassured myself.

A few days and nights happened the same, the snake crawled out early in the morning, in the hot afternoon it crawled into the tunnel, fortunately, the soldiers went to investigate outside, so no one knew there was a snake in the tunnel except me.

In the early morning, the enemy's 155mm cannons were heavily fired at our battlefield.
"Boom...bang" – continous explosions and some were very close to the army tunnel. The smell of artillery powder mixed with thick dust, our troops were ordered to attack to break the siege, and at the same time urgently avoided enemy's cannons changing lanes.
I led the 1st Company to fight the left wing, just crawled a few meters, suddenly the black snake crawled very quickly from nowhere, it raised its high head, its tongue stuck out. I realized; it was the ordinary snake crawling into the cellar for a few days. I was holding a K54 gun about to shoot it, for some reason, the snake was still holding high its

Homeland: Song Hien Ward, Cao Bang City, Cao Bang Province
Member of Literature and Arts Association of Vietnamese Ethnic Minorities
Member of Vietnam Writers's Association
Member of Literature and Arts Association of Cao Bang Province
Literature works published: 20 poetry and short/medium story collections; And some of them were republished many times

head, ready to jump straight on me.

At the same time, I heard the enemy shouting very close, so I signaled the soldiers to crawl to the right quickly. "Boom...bang", right after that, there were two ear-piercing explosions, right where I just met the snake. "Wow...god ". Smoke and dust rolled up and down into the air, covering the soldiers on the ground. "Is anyone hurt?"

I asked softly "Report to the Captain no one got hurt". The replies were

Every Child lifeline /DEMO GOG international magazine

Vietnamese Prose Page

short enough for to hear. How about the snake? Or was it hit by a mine? I could not hide surprise: How did the snake know it was dangerous to stop our troops? There, the iron helmets loomed in the dust, bringing me back to reality. "Boom…. bang"; "bang"; "tack… tack…tack".

The sound of the enemy's guns, individual mortars and AR15s spitted bullets continously with the responding sounds of AK, AK 47, RPK, B40… of the Laos army. Badly explosions, burning smell from gunpowders, red dust rolled up dozens of meters high, erasing my worry about the snake, I aimed the K54 at the chest of the man who was pointing his personal mortar at our soldiers.

The enermy soldier jerked and collapsed, his personal mortar hitting the ground. Until late afternoon that our troops broke through the encirclement and escaped behind the Chum Plain. Later, I heard the scout soldiers telling: The soldier was crawling in the last position, encountered a rather large black snake, raised its head nearby, it seemed that it was about to bite him, so he quickly grabbed a stone and threw it at the snake, maybe the stone hit the mine planted nearby and exploded!

Over the past few decades, many ups and downs in my life, especially soldiers like me, due to a piece of mortar stuck in my chest, although treated, my health is weaker than before.

A year later when I returned home and continued to work in the Northwest Military Region, the story of the snake always haunted me, throughout the whole battle in Laos, and even when he returned home, I did not tell him anyone about the story of that mysterious snake. I always remember that black snake that saved me and the Laos soldiers thirty years ago...

- Did the Snake know that there were mines? Tung asked
- I did not know…but that was the truth! Father's voice is deep: I know there is a very big Cobra near bamboo bush at the end of our garden, yesterday I noticed, it seemed that Lan and Uncle Lin stalking to catch it, right?
- Yes, last afternoon, Uncle Lin also saw it in the bamboo bush…it's longer than an adult's arm span, it's so big! Lan said.
- Uncle Lin and I are going to catch that Snake for meat or sell it? Father still speaks in his low voice.
- Uncle Lin said that if the snaked get caught, he would sell to the old fat Tuc, the wine shop owner in the market, at least two or three hundred thousand … Lan tald innocently.
- According to me, you'd better telling Uncle Lin not to catch it, let it go! Snakes love to hunt Rats, it's also useful, as long as humans don't hunt and tease it, it won't harm humans. Father's voice is still low.
-Yes, the story you just told about the Snake made me think differently about this animal! From now on, I won't catch it again. Lan said.
- Yes, don't kill them! Protect the animals...even the Snakes! when I was in Laos, if it weren't that Snake, I might not be able returned! Father sighs.
- Come on, let's all eat potatoes and go to sleep! It's late. Mother says softly.

The whole family happily sat around a basket of boiled sweet potatoes. They are are very sweet. Tung looks at the blue sky, thousands of sparkling stars. The moon in the middle of the month is round near Phia Oac mountain in the distance, radiating clear light on all things. Tung suddenly gazes the big bamboo bush at the end of the garden where the Cobra staying, he thought to himself: don't be afraid, Lan and Uncle Lin won't catch you anymore!

Every Child lifeline /DEMO GOG international magazine
Vietnamese Prose Page

THE SECRET OF ATTRACTION
Written by Vo Chi Nhat

Despite having loads of books, I just read a few of them. Only if I could read more, but my work schedule keeps me hectic. Reading has become my habit with no doubts. I pick what to read based on my preferences - whether it's my favorite genre, a book cover that catches my eye, a writer I really know or from a country I love. I've digested books by Agatha Christie, Conan Doyle, John Sandford, Philip Roth... and they've all inspired me to start writing on my own. I always tell myself, "Just start writing and you'll eventually finish." But the problem is, I tend to forget my ideas once I actually get started. My teacher used to say that's certainly a good thing because each story I write ends up being different from the last. To combat my forgetfulness, I make sure to jot down ideas on paper or on my phone whenever I can't sit at a table.

I started reading when I was in 7th grade. At first, my mom didn't want me to read because she was worried I would "live in a virtual world." So, I would read during recess at school or secretly at my grandpa's place. It all began with famous detective Conan comics and then I moved on to Sherlock Holmes short stories. I fell head over heels for detective stories and started practicing my writing skills.

According to Thomas Mann, a novel's scope and ambition are just as important as its stylistic techniques and narrative strategy. Sartre teaches us that words are powerful

and that a well-crafted novel, screenplay, or essay has the ability to change history. So, as a writer, I believe that every word should be valued and used wisely. Have you ever wondered why detective stories are rarely written and widely translated in our country? It's interesting how this genre is so popular in Western countries like England, France, and Belgium. They even have monuments named after it!

Ever since I published my story collection, Ash And Cinder, I've been getting a lot of questions from readers asking me where I come up with all these ideas for my stories. Honestly, I don't even think about it. Every day, all over the world, crimes are happening and innocent people are being victimized. Some pay the price, while others get away with it. That's where the role of a detective writer comes in. We try to figure out how the crimes are committed and seek justice for the victims on the page. As writer Nguyen Tuan calls it, the "white execution ground". But detective stories are not just cautionary tales or rehashed crime stories. They need to be "reconstructed" from real cases, following my own principle of using 7 parts real and 3 parts added elements. Like in Ash And Cinder, or from a familiar saying like "thief meets the old woman". I have this story called Dung xem do la bay, or there's *"Sherlock Holmes Wears A Skirt"*, for example.

A good detective story can be summed up in two words: "tension and surprise", and a few other elements. It starts with an intriguing puzzle that challenges the reader's intellect. And of course, it must be fun and have a surprising ending. The reader has to keep reading until the very last page to find out who the culprit is. And if they can't help but exclaim in delight, then it's a successful detective story. Before I start writing, I read a lot. And I also need a good and relatable case to build an attractive storyline. The characters I create have to be unique, with their own backgrounds and distinctive writing styles.

Every Child lifeline /DEMO GOG international magazine

Vietnamese Prose Page

They need to have their own methods of investigation and engage in intelligent dialogue. But there's one thing they all have in common – they have to be knowledgeable. Only then can they break the mold.

Another thing about detective stories is that they're a global genre. So I often use global comparisons and symbols. But what's more important is the identity aspect. The players in this genre are engaged in a "high identity war". Why? Because it's our thing, our own flavor, so that readers don't get bored. So even though it's a detective story, the setting, weather, and customs are different. It's like the spice, the seasoning that adds flavor to the work. Just like how the historical detective story, *"The Name Of The Rose"*, once caused a sensation.

When you're reading detective stories, you gotta pay attention to every little detail, even the tiniest ones. 'Cause nothing happens by chance, you know? Like, the character's mood, a big rose garden with no bees buzzing around, or a scarf wrapped around a middle-aged guy's neck in the middle of summer in Cu Chi. These are the things that make you stop and think, you know? 'Cause sometimes, those small, seemingly harmless details can end up being super important to the main character's problem.

The structure of a detective story is like a triangle with three sides. Every detail in the story has a purpose, and there's no extra stuff. And you can bet that detective stories always have a big, dramatic ending, just like the bottom of a triangle. The dialogue can get pretty long too. Our detective predecessors, like Agatha Christie, have been doing it this way for a long time. I've been trying to find a way to make the ending less intense, but it ain't easy at all.

The more lonely I feel, the more I write. I write when I'm both happy and sad. Mostly short stories. You see, people these days are so caught up in the daily grind, they don't have time to relax and have fun. That's why I write these clever, lighthearted detective stories. They give readers a chance to enjoy literature and have some entertainment while solving puzzles, kinda like biting into a juicy summer pear. And as long as there are cases that keep me on edge, I'll keep on writing...

Oh, and there's a few more secrets too. But I'll only reveal them to a certain extent, just like the title says: the secret of attraction!

Vo Chi Nhat was born and raised in Cu Chi district, Ho Chi Minh City. He officially started his writing career in 2013 and has been a member of the Ho Chi Minh City Writers Association since 2017. In 2016, he released his first historical novel and then shifted his focus to writing police and crime stories, which aligns with his chosen career path. He believes that a writer should begin with what they are best at.

Currently, he's wrapping up the book series "Middleman and the crime" featuring the central character Ha "chili". Ha "chili" portrays a real colleague who has "chocolate skin" and a "voice like a spoon scraping the bottom of a bowl", but possesses a genuine passion for the typically mundane field of crime investigation, which is often seen as unsuitable for women.

His works have been translated and published in both domestic and international magazines.

Translated by L. H. Trong Nghia

Every Child lifeline /DEMO GOG international magazine

Vietnamese Poetry Page

Short Bio: S Afrose (Sabiha Afrose from Bangladesh); has been writing since Aug-2020. Poetry is her best friend. Some of her published poetry books available on Amazon Worldwide 🌐: Thanks Dear God, Poetic Essence, Reflection of Mind, Glittering Hopes, Angels Smile, Tiny Garden of Words, Dancing Alphabet, Artistic Muse, Essence of Love, Dear Children, Haunted Site, Woman, A Little Fantasy, The Butterfly, Lion's Roar, The Magical Quill etc.

Can reach her at afrosewritings@outlook.com, YouTube: S Afrose * Muse of Writes * (@safrose_poetic_arts), Facebook page: Muse of Words by S Afrose.

Pray and Pray

This is omnipotent for all of us,
Pray and pray for the peaceful earth.
Today earth is in uncontrolled ocean,
So many strikes, so many bleeding hearts.

How can we bear this time?
How can we live with peaceful hub?
How can we speak for the desired lane?
Who will help, dear friends?

Humanity and humanity!
Fabricated the mind's eyes.
Need to accept the lane of love,
We want to hear all peaceful urges.

Love and love for the earth,
We know we will we must do.
It's the time to wake up,
We will hold hands of beloved ones.

The magic of mankind!
Need to shower the petals of heart.
We know we can If we want,
As this is the prime concern.

Should be or not
This is not a fault,
Let me hold this time
Pray and pray for the desired universe.

To dear Almighty all the time,
Let us keep the mind's urges,
We don't want to cry anymore,
We want to live with all dear ones.

Copyright © S Afrose, Bangladesh
30th Oct-23

Every Child lifeline /DEMO GOG international magazine
Vietnamese Poetry Page

Existence of Nanoscience in Vedic Culture

Nanoscience is emerging science which deals with characterization or synthesis of materials at the nanometer-scale which has emerged in the 21st century. Nanoscience has an important role in medication, especially in non-herbal medicine preparation [2]. However, similar knowledge also exists since the Vedic period (circa 1500 – 500 BCE) within the Indian subcontinent in the field of Ayurveda, the traditional system of Hindu medicine. Ayurveda consists of two parts, the physician and the medicine.

Ayurveda is defined as a collection of medicinal knowledge which deals with "Science of Life" within ages. Nanotechnology is a recent innovation belonging to the 21st century within the industrial revolution and plays a vital role in re-engineering the man-made world. Nanotechnology has created great waves of innovation from engineering to medicine [6]. Although Ayurveda is ancient and Nanotechnology is modern, this forms a deep relationship. In initial days, "Nanotechnology" was termed via Richard Feynman and Norio Taniguchi in 1974 AD. There are many examples that indicate the presence and role of nanomaterials since ancient times.

The preparation of drugs associated with Ayurveda are e Kashthaushadhies (herbal preparations) and Rasaushadhi (herb-bio-mineral-metallic preparations). The behavior of Rasaushadhi are quick action, low dose, long shelf life. These have helped meet the demands of patients as well as pharmaceutical companies [8]. Along with these drugs, some more properties can be acquired via Shodhana, Marana, Sathipattana, Kupipakwa, and Pottali in a strict sequence. Within these, Marana (Incineration/Calcination) is a needed procedure in Nanotechnology. Marana changes the physicochemical behavior of a metal or mineral, i.e., by reducing particle size, as needed for therapeutic purposes. Shodhana (detoxification) is the initial step of Marana which is defined as the purification of materials (metals and minerals). After this step, Bhavana, uncontaminated metal is titrating by distinct herbal juice till a doughy mass is obtained. Chakrika Nirmana (palletization) is next process to form Chakrika (pellets) for drying by doughy mass. After that, dry flat pellets are placed on another earthen saucer one by one, which is covered by mud-smeared cloth and left to dry. Such an arrangement is known as Puta Yantra. The Puta Yantra is then subjected to Puta. Puta describes a heating process for a specific period of time, which is a final step for Marana. After this, pellets are examined and collected, and ground into fine powder. The procedure is being repeated till wished physicochemical and biological properties are analyzed within the material.

The usability of metal-minerals formulation for therapeutic purposes is known as Bhasma (ashes), which are observed in Ayurveda like Jasda Bhasma (Zinc), Loha Bhasma (Iron), Rajat Bhasma (Silver), Tamra Bhasma (Copper) [10]. Ashes of such minerals are frequently observed as medicines whose categories include Abarka (Mica), Muga (Coral), Sipi (Oyster shell), Moti (pearl shell) and whose traditional technique, known as bhasmikaran, does not need highly sophisticated equipment and is not a health hazard.

Herbo-metal preparations are highly regarded in Ayurveda, where particle sizes in the range 10-50 nm are classified as biomedicine in metal-based or carbon-based forms up to a size limit of 100 nm. Hence, the above-described Bhasma is known as a bio-medicine having varied applications. For example, Jasda Bhasma is applied for curing tuberculosis and diabetes. Acidity, cirrhosis can be cured by Tamra Bhasma (Copper ash) & Swarna Bhasma (Gold Ash) easily cures rheumatoid arthritis. Various additives, the duration of the reaction, and temperature play vital roles in a major impact on the efficiency of Nanomedicine (Bhasma). Gold Nanoparticles (AuNP) play an active role in the drug delivery system. Hence, the roles of Gold (Au), Silver (Ag), and Copper (Cu) are being analyzed with a focus on the treatment of many diseases in the modern era.

\In recent days, nanotechnology plays a great role for drug delivery systems due to its-self targeting property & its size. Examples of nanoparticles are nanospheres or nano-capsules. Nanoparticles also play the role carriers for other drugs. The applications of Nanotechnology increase bioavailability, the bioactivity of phytomedicine, and the trapping of phytomedicines, diagnosis, bioimaging technique. It has also been used as a sunscreen lotion that blocks unwanted Ultraviolet rays or protects against skin damage.

The future of combining research of Nanotechnology and traditional herbal medicine opens the opportunity of designing a drug having high bioavailability profile and lower toxicity which has a great role in the future medication era.

Every Child lifeline /DEMO GOG international magazine

Vietnamese Poetry Page

Steps to Success (Story of Makhfiratkhon Abdurakhmonova) Makhfiratkhon Abdurakhmonova, born in 2004, possessed an extraordinary passion for learning and a burning desire to make a positive impact on the world. Makhfiratkhon's journey towards greatness began at a tender age when she discovered her love for the English language. At just four years old, she started teaching English to children in her neighborhood. Her natural talent and enthusiasm for teaching quickly caught the attention of international educators. By the age of eight, Makhfiratkhon had already achieved an impressive list of accomplishments. She was certified as a B2 level English teacher according to CEFR standards in Uzbekistan. Her thirst for knowledge led her to obtain various international certifications, including International ESOL-B2 and SAYLOR ACADEMY-C1. Not only was Makhfiratkhon an academic prodigy, but she also excelled in extracurricular activities. She became a member of numerous international organizations and attended over 50 conferences worldwide. Her dedication and hard work did not go unnoticed, as she received recognition as a global youth ambassador. Makhfiratkhon's dreams continued to come true as she won scholarships to prestigious universities such as North Texas University, Barry University, and St.Johns University. She was awarded the University Incentive Scholarship, which further fueled her determination to succeed academically. In addition to her academic pursuits, Makhfiratkhon was actively involved in philanthropic endeavors. She served as a Child Rescue Ambassador for IQRA Foundation and as a Child Advisor for Glory Future Foundation. Her passion for environmental conservation led her to become an ambassador for the renowned organization 'Greenpeace.' Makhfiratkhon's achievements extended beyond academics and philanthropy; she was also recognized for her skills in diplomacy and international affairs. She participated in the Asia World Model United Nations (AWMUN) Offline Conference, where she excelled and won an internship opportunity. As a Fellow member of ERU and a member of the ISRES, Makhfiratkhon was always at the forefront of global issues. Her dedication to making a positive impact on society led her to translate several books and become an ambassador for various organizations, including SGAP Leaders and Global Friends Club. Her passion for education also shone through as she completed courses from prestigious universities such as the University of California and Stanford University. Makhfiratkhon's commitment to self-improvement knew no bounds, as she also attended conferences in Thailand, Malaysia, and the United Arab Emirates as a delegate of 'Best Diplomats.' Despite her numerous accomplishments, Makhfiratkhon remained humble and grounded. She volunteered for organizations such as 'Quyosh Nuri' and worked tirelessly as an official member of IAAC and Gurukshetra Foundation. With each passing day, Makhfiratkhon's influence grew stronger. She became an ambassador for IHRC in Uzbekistan and coordinated various initiatives aimed at promoting peace and human rights. Her dedication to her country's youth led her to become the Country President of Iqra Foundation Global in Uzbekistan. Makhfiratkhon's passion for writing bore fruit when she authored her book titled "A Shining Star." Through this book, she hoped to inspire others to chase their dreams relentlessly. As time went on, Makhfiratkhon continued to add feathers to her cap. She became a member of Juntos Por Las Letras and UN-ONGO, further solidifying her status as a global leader. Makhfiratkhon's story is one that inspires countless individuals around the world. Her unwavering determination, thirst for knowledge, and commitment to making a positive difference have made her a true shining star. Through her dreams and aspirations, Makhfiratkhon continues to prove that with hard work and dedication, anything is possible.

Mukhlisa Bakhodirova was born in Uzbekistan and is the student of Ferghana State University. Now, she is the member and ambassador of a lot of international organizations.

Every Child lifeline /DEMO GOG international magazine

Vietnamese Poetry Page

В «Доме детского и юношеского творчества» города Курчатове области Абай в целях развития творческих талантов молодого поколения работает литературный кружок "Лира". Руководитель литературного кружка Кумарханова Айнур работает с детьми в этом направлении. На сегодняшний день эти ребята уже стали призерами международных и республиканских конкурсов. Их произведения были опубликованы в журнале «SMILE" в Узбекистане на узбекском языке, в журнале «Дружба народов» в Таджикистане, в республиканском журнале "Детски мир". Что бы прочитать стихи юных талантов Муратхан Айым, Сериков Зейн, Турсынбек Нургалым мы предлагаем на страницах журнала. Наша цель направлена на популяризацию детской литературы в мире.

АЙНУР КУМАРХАНОВА Поэт, переводчик. Переводите с разных азиатских языков мира. Пишет стихи на казахском и русском языках. Родился 10 марта 1983 года в Казахстане в городе Семипалатинске. Живет в Курчатово. Автор 3 книг. Победитель республиканских международных конкурсов. Мировой поэт.

Ана
Анам менің-өмірім,
Жаксы көрем бәрінен!
Қалдырмаймын конілін,
Бакытты етем әлі мен!
Анам менің-жүрегім,
Тастамаймын ешқашан,
Анам менің-әлемім,
Құрметтеймін әркашан!
Анам менің-шуағым,
Дүниеге әкелген!
Амандығын сұрадым.
Бәрін сатып әперген!
Бесік әнін жырлаған.
Әлдилеген анашым!
Түн ұйқысын ұрлагам,
Еркелеткен баласын..

Сериков Зейин
Дом детского и юношеского творчества
г Курчатова

Казахстан

Келіп қалды күз мезгілі
Жапырақтар түсіп жатыр
Күн ызғарлы, суытады
Құстар самғап ұшып жатыр

Сарғылт тартты жердің жүзі
Көп сағынтып күзім келді
Бұлт қалыңдап жауын жауды
Сол жаңбырмен жер лайланды

Айналаны тұман басты
Көңіл күйді жабырқатты
Ауа райы бұзылғанды
Күз осылай құбылғанды

Мұратхан Айым
Дом детского и юношеского творчества
г Курчатов
Казахстан

Ұстаз
Ұстаз деген адалдыққа үйретер
Білімімен бойды ақылмен билетер
Ұстаз деген керек екен адамға
Өз сәулесін шашу үшін ғаламға!

Ұстаз деген болғанымен әр түрлі
Қиындыққа қалдырмайды әр кімді
Ұстаз үлгі әр оқушы үшінде
Ұлағаттық жасырулы ісінде

Ұстаз болу менің басты арманым,
Біліммен нұрланса екен жан жағым
Еңбегі де ол адамның қиындау
Сан сынақпен шыңдап өтер талғамын

Ұстаздық ол талап етеді сабырды,
Ұстаздар да сен білмитін бар үлгі
Өз алдыңда мен басымды иемін,
Ей ұстазым, ей кемеңгер қалірлі!

Тұрсынбек Нұрғалым

Дом детского и юношеского творчества г Курчатова
Казахстан

Every Child lifeline /DEMO GOG international magazine

Vietnamese Poetry Page

To be a Writer

To be a Writer is to take on various roles,
the first of which is that
of an observer
beholding the ever-changing world
with all its hues and shades
which swell and spread, which blend and scatter,
becoming the infinite inkwell into which
a pen may dip and give birth to the words
that carry forth the fragments of
the most perplexing and complex of essences
so that the readers may have a sample of what
life has to offer;

The second of which is that
of a listener
experiencing the voices found in everything,
the chirps of birds, the roars of winds,
the taps of rain, the sighs of leaves,
the cries of newborns mixed with those of joy,
the sounds of mourning dyed with chants of grief,
and many more, and countless more,
each one a symphony in its own right
that when combined,
a most intriguing orchestra is birthed,
which the Writer, as a listener, strives to transcribe
so that the audience may have a taste of what
the tides of Life can bring;

The third of which is that
of a connoisseur
forever learning to appreciate the fragrances
and flavors of the mortal world,
forever honing one's own craft
and ever chasing after knowledge in a haze
with the blazing hope that
wisdom may be gained,
and enlightenment may yet be reached,
an endless journey wherein one road leads
to others in a labyrinthine wonder that is Life,
and on that tireless pilgrimage,
a skillful Writer may persuade, invite, inspire
others to come along
and together yearn to catch a glimpse
of the Truth that lies beyond the confine of
mortality.

Shruti Singh, a poetic alchemist, forging emotions into eloquence, born to breathe life into words.

BRUTAL TRUTH

What's the age?
Just a number...most of us would say..
What's the height?
Just a measurement...calculative sign..
What's the costume?
Just the cloth...wrapped around..
What's the colour?
Just a shade...as per the region..
What's the religion?
Just a faith...aligning mass together..
Why beating the bush?
Just trying to find...the reasons behind..
What you exactly trying?
Just finding the reasons behind...this brutality..
When n where these men get audacity?
To RAPE a life...
Be it KID, GIRL, LADY or somebody's WIFE..
What exact mentality turns them shady?
Above stated traits were reported,
As a reason of their hunting..
How far you pals being tolerating???
Precisely decision is awaiting..

Ngo Binh Anh Khoa is a teacher of English in Ho Chi Minh City, Vietnam. In his free time, he enjoys reading fiction and writing speculative poetry. His poems have appeared in Weirdbook, Star*Line, Spectral Realms, and other venues. He also writes haiku on occasions, many of which have received honorable mentions and awards in various contests in the US, the UK, Japan, Canada, and elsewhere.

Every Child lifeline /DEMO GOG international magazine

Free microphone

Nature is the Mother of all beauties and home of unlimited charms. Without it, all genres are foxy with the absence of ornaments and this is something which is a priceless boon as well as the bountiful blessings of the Almighty. It exists in the literary works of every culture. It is the backbone of plots and also helps us to learn about the original image. The world is endowed with rich beauteous natural resources which can all be inspirations to compose lovely poetry and prose and to even be the eternal subjects of masterpieces. As the great poet, John Keats says: *"The poetry of the earth never died"*. Shakespeare also stated before that: *"One touch of nature makes the whole world kin"*.

With the increasing threats of global warming it's our responsibility to take care of NATURE.
Nature is the soul of the worldly body. How can we as humans help nurture nature in our own little ways? Nature shows peace, calmness, power, and strength as well. A few writers consider it as a path for independence. The ancient people took it with their own perspectives. For instance, the Earth refers to a woman whose anger brings earthquakes.
William Black also talked about its importance and said: "The tree which moves some to tears of joy is in the eyes of others only a green thing that stands in the way. Some see nature all ridicule and deformity... and some scarce see nature at all. But to the eyes of the man of imagination, nature is imagination itself."
In poetry, nature is a religion for Romantic Poets. There is pleasure that exists in it, and they discover life secrets in her. William Wordsworth seeks God in nature and said: *"Come forth into the light of things, let nature be your teacher."* He further said in his poem 'Tintern Abbey'- *"Nature never did betray the heart that loved her"*.
S. T. Coleridge perceives nature with supernatural portions. He stated: *"For he on honey-dew hath fed, and drank the milk of Paradise."* John Keats the great Romantic poet says: *"No bird has left in the world, which has not left an influence on his mind"*. For Keats Nature is his best friend.
Both writers and artists use sky as the symbolism of calmness and the dwelling of gods, it also shows the Divine forces. The blue sky is portrayed for happiness and serenity. The sky at night presents the picture of death and evil forces and the heavy cloud formations bring sadness to the core.
The lovely rainbow after the rain connotes hope and a brand new tomorrow; a solemn promise of the Divine. Using nature in Literature would be like a Good Man who is 'Hard to Find'.
O' Connor perceives that there is nothing in the sky, it's religious imagery in it. It means that there is no God, and that humanity cannot hope for salvation. Sun is another common symbol which is used in Mythology. It gives life to everyone. It also shows power, Divine forces as well. The sunrise shows hope whereas, the sunset exposes the end of life. For example, in the novel *Klara and the Sun*, 'Klara can see outside the window to watch the rising and setting of the Sun, which she believes gives her nourishment.'
Water is also a traditional sign which is used in different works. It depicts rebirth, power, chaos, and danger. Sea also shows life. This is also a symbol of the rites of baptism that washes away sins. Water in the novel *Crime and Punishment* comes to represent life and renewal and has different meanings for different characters. For positive characters, it connotes life and growth. Whereas, water terrifies negative characters with its threat of death.
Another literary device using nature is the woods. Woods are always dangerous for human and people believe dark forces live among them, therefore they express being lost, endangered, and mysterious as well.
"I went to the woods because I wanted to live deliberately, I wanted to live deep and suck out all the marrow of life, to put to rout all that was not life and not when I had come to die, discover that I had not lived." - Henry David Thoreau
Nature is the most vital boon of God. It fulfills our desires. With the increasing threats of global warming it's our responsibility to take care of it. It's our home and many creatures live and thrive for our benefit. God creates all things for us. Everything like the sun, the moon, trees, and animals. She provides us food, oxygen, water, shelter, and medicine as well.
There is no doubt that we should nurture Mother Nature because she does protect us, too. Because of its love we are alive, motivated, and healthy. Our universe presents paradise. Human beings are making progress and trying to reach other planets but they have ignored our only home. Due to our greedy behavior, we are spoiling its purity. If we don't take care and preserve it, the priceless gift of the Almighty, we will be the killers of our future generations. Unfortunately we are unaware of the dangers of not protecting nature and so we reap what we sow.

, P. B. Shelley' writes in "The Flower That Smiles To-Day":
"The flower that smiles to-day
To-morrow dies;
All that we wish to stay
Tempts and then flies.
What is this world's delight?
Lightning that mocks the night,
Brief even as bright."

Shahid Abbas is a multi-awarded International Author and Poet from Karapla, Tandlianwala Faisalabad Pakistan. He is the author of "Words from Nature" and the co-author of "We Speak In Syllables". His works were also featured in various international anthologies and diverse literary platforms both in print and online. Shahid's works were already translated into 10 different languages.

Every Child lifeline /DEMO GOG international magazine

Free microphone

Rainbowed Masterpiece

You reside
inside and outside of me
You are the Earth;
Reborn and calm
After the storm.

The storm washes me clean
To paint the rainbow
Transforming me into a masterpiece.
The waves are now still
Writing stories of valour in me.

The sun smiles in me
Taking pride that I am able to
defeat the storm each time.
The Earth turns green and magical
Standing the test of time.

Priyalakshmi Gogoi is from Assam, India. A Teacher by profession and a poet by passion. Her poems have been published in popular newspapers in her city and in blogs, Instagram, editorial, e-magazines. She has also co-authored few national and international Anthologies. She has been awarded several times for winning Poetry contests in various literary platforms and has been conferred with prestigious awards. She is also a World English Saino Writer and a Gogyohka writer. She has been awarded the 75th Independence Day Literary Honor on 15th August, 2021and India Independence Day Global Literary Honors 2021-22 jointly given by Motivational Strips and Gujarat Sahitya Academy in "Recognition of Exhibiting Literary Brilliance Par Global Standards". She has also been conferred with Rabindranath Tagore Memorial Honour, 2022 by Motivational Strips and Dept of Culture, Govt of Seychelles and its journal SIPAY.

Every Child lifeline / DEMO GOG international magazine

Free microphone

BEATITUDE

My eyes blinked over and over again,
With an amazement how nature is a beatitude.
In one solitary journey to Shillong ,
I was in a close proximity with such a fascination.

The journey was long for a vagrant ,
Weaving emotions to cherish the scenery in a lake front.
The tribal women seemed so beautiful ,
Khasi and Gora are their origin and so delightful.

The Don Bosco museum left me mesmerised ,
It's skyscraper and the figurines;
With artefacts impregnated my instincts.
The beautiful cliffs and lakes enriched my imaginations,
The cleanest village in the world Mawsynram ,
And the Dawki river in Meghalaya is a terrific spiritual strum .

Amb. Somdatta Mitra

She lives in her present never forgetting her past. Her past resonates her scars and diabolical moments which augmented her to enliven her poems with her weapon , the pen. A postgraduate in English from India , Amb. Somdatta Mitra , always battled against social injustices , treachery and discriminations through her poems. Magnifying the prophet in her , she promulgated in human rights activities through her literary works. Innumerable accolades in paintings , poetry recitals , published poems and short stories , articles and quotes has bestowed her with a global honour in each spectrum. As an extrovert , she harmoniously preaches and believes in " Peace and solidarity ". Her friendship ties in the world literary arena has divulged in world records and ornated her journey with divine accolades and luminaries. She has a diploma in computer Desk Top Publishing and a diploma in Commercial Art. She has completed more than 1000 anthologies. Her poetry book by the name " Unheard Voices " is still under publication.

Every Child lifeline / DEMO GOG international magazine

Free microphone

The Sun

When the sun appears with its light,
Darkness ends,the day becomes bright
Like a fireball flying in space,
It is unparalleled in it's grace.
Always it keeps track of time,
Loves goodness and hates crime.
Moves slowly towards the destination,
Faces problems and finds solution.
Aha!Neither cries nor slumbers,
Cool in winters,hot in summers,
Sleeps on time and wakes on time,
Ripens the crops and melts the rime.
Dries wet things with its heat,
Teaches children never to cheat.

By
Muhammad Ishaq Abbasi
PAKISTAN

I Saw A Dream

The air was fragrant with light drizzle.
 I got lost in the memories of my childhood.
And the cool air made me sleep deeply.
Then I saw something like this.
That I reached such a place,
flying with a cloud.
Where I was shown something ,
Had never seen before.
The voices of peace and tranquility were everywhere.
There were vines, date palms,
And all kinds of trees.
And beneath them flowed streams,
Of milk,honey and sweet water.
There was such jam liquor,
That did not spoil the mind.
Silk beds were laid out for relaxation.
There were tall, fair-skinned ,
and beautiful nymphs.
Green birds were flying everywhere.
There was good health and eternal youth.
 All kinds of pure food were available.
There was such a fragrance that,
Perfumed the heart and mind.
I asked shyly
 Whose place is this?
So was told
Those who care about,
 the rights of the people,
Make peace between angry people,
 And treat parents well.
 My forehead became sweaty,
And my dream was shattered.

By
Muhammad Ishaq Abbasi

Dr. Muhammad Ishaq Abbasi is an eminent poet and Master trainer.He has a deep love for Nature. It is his hobby to help someone in difficult times. It is his Nature to support the weak against the strong. Humility is the food of his soul. He was born on Monday, November 16, 1975, in Dhok Morian, a lush village Khuian Tehsil Kahuta District Rawalpindi Pakistan. He is the fourth of five siblings. When he was three years old,his mother fell into a ravine and was hospitalized for six months before dying. The journey from childhood to adolescence was spent without the wings of a mother, which is difficult to describe in words. Without mother's love, colorfulness of childhood faded and the newborn's face was the abode of mother's kisses. And on the cheeks where mother's affection was dancing There, drops of tears falling from the shores of the eyes formed spots Father who was a military officials. He left no stone unturned. Grandmother who was 80 years old. Due to physical and visual impairment, She used to cooked wheat bread on the inverted iron round vessel which was black but had to be eaten under compulsion. At that time, all the houses in the village were made of mud and stones. When it rained, the houses would start dripping and he would sometimes move his bed to one side and sometimes to the other. He got his early education from Government High School, Salamber. There was a school bag of woolen cloths, plastic sleepers and plain cloth to wear. The two brothers used to pick up his school bag when they went to and from school and help him in educational matters. Because of them, he is standing at this place today. On Sunday,they would all go to the fountain to wash their clothes. Passed matriculation examination from Government High School Narar Passed D.com exam from Government Commercial College, Kahuta. He passed BA and MA examinations from University of The Punjab as regular candidate. Later he passed B.Ed from Allama Iqbal Open University Islamabad and M.Ed from Sargodha University. Honorary doctorate in English literature from International Academy of Culture and Literature He started writing poetry in 2007. He wrote mostly poems on nature. He participated in international literary poetry competitions and won more than 150 international awards. At the national level, he also wrote poems for children who have been awarded certificates of appreciation by the National Book Foundation.He also raise his voice through pen for peace in the world. The following is a list of the international organizations he is part of Oxygen Pen.Genesis World writers Community. Iqra Foundation. Literary Creations .World literary forum for peace and Human Rights.Pen wonder International.The Dream Of Equality Pakistan.Literature Archive Bangladesh.The passion Of Poetry.Poetry for Humanity & Nature.World peace of poets.World Of Poets. Peace and Love Inkers Society.The International Poetry.Taifas Literary Magazine. Poetry and literature world vision.DEMO GOG. Words:A Renaissance.The Poetry center.Realms of poems.Poems and stories. ILA Magazine.Motivational strips.World kids book poetic.United Poets and heart.Flladi poetic.Sparking Quil.world spiritual love and peace Humanity literary Foundation.The Temple of impeccable writers.The Dream Of Equality Nigeria.Elite Arab Creative Union. Ever Child lifeline Foundation. His poems have been published in various anthologies and Newspaper of the world, for example.Women the society backbone. The Poetic Soul.Peace and Love Inkers Around the World.Midnight in the Garden of Peace.The Mask,You,Mari maa,Alone,Chuceberrirs Garden,A Bouquet of Triple colours.Awskener of hidden potential, Amazing Gardener,The Global Nation World Record book Hyperpoem.

Every Child lifeline /DEMO GOG international magazine

Free microphone

I DREAMT ONLY

1. I only dreamt of crossing the seas
Flying in the air , moving with a breeze .
I am not able to walk on the earth even in
Thirties
I only dreamt of reading the books of literature
Philosophy , politics and each religion
But until thirties I have known the names of
None.
I only dreamt of buying an expensive car
And building a beautiful house
But until thirties I couldn't buy a trap for a mouse
I only dreamt of marrying a rich , beautiful and pious woman
But until thirties not even a black faced , poor and rude One proposed me for fun
I only dreamt of becoming a doctor, a journalist or a pilot
But until thirties I couldn't become a janitor in any department
O such is my lot .

SHAFKAT AZIZ HAJAM, is a poet, reviewer and co author from India Kashmir. He is the author of two children poetry books titled as The cuckoo's voice and the canary's voice. His poems have been published in international anthologies like wheel song anthology UK based, Prodigy, Inner Child Press International etc .He is also a private school teacher

Every Child lifeline /DEMO GOG international magazine

Free microphone

"Please don't fall for me"

Yeah ! I am different from what you think ,
So ,Don't fall in love with me, Don't try to learn why I'm like this ,
coz I have trust issues I won't share it with you,
If you try to gain my trust ,
And if I fell on your kindness,
If I tell you the episodes of my life,you'll fall harder.
Please then ,
Don't fall in love with me, Cause I'm very sensitive , Every action of mine is going to make you question your ability,
 Cause I'm loyal in every way, I will move mountains for you,
 If I love you hard
If I make time for you
 If I feel you need my attention.
Don't fall in love with me, Cause I'm going to push you through all edges and over all boulders than anyone in life,
 I see things what others don't,
 I know what your capable of and know your potentials.
Don't fall in love with me, Cause I will be the last person standing where you left,
with my arms wide open, believing in you
still lifting you up,
 when the whole world stops trusting you.
And lastly, don't fall in love with me cause,
I know you more then
 you know yourself.

"Emptiness makes me alive "
An emptiness inside me
 Which will never leave me I've done a lot
  loved a lot,
  given a lot
  worked hard without even any care
 No matter will be paid or not for my extra work.
 Yeah, All I ever wanted was an appreciation,
 a remembrance,
 a thought from a loyal and honest heart,
All I wanted was respect and dignity.
All I ever wanted was for people to understand me,
to support me
 guide me if I was wrong,
All I ever wanted was for people to love me
 not betray or back stab
but, all in vain,
Oh! I forgot I live in the world filled with cowards and hypocrites.
 I forgot all are sugar coated will be true to you only when you are successful
When you can give benefits to them,
Well no matter what it is?
 I dont think I can ever change who I am?
so love me or leave me, it's your choice.
Well I think, emptiness is the only thing which I love the most....
cause it's the only way to me stay alive....

Ms. Pratikshya Paudel a young and inspiring Dental Hygienist from Syangja, Nepal is poetess by motivation. Apart from her professional obligations, she loves writing a lot. Ms. Pratikshya is an anchor who loves listening to people and their stories. She loves reciting poetries. She has immensely contributed in the field of literature by interviewing icons and luminaries of literature from different nations under the banner of Swopnil Literary Society. She also likes social activities and more importantly she loves being charitable in helping less privileged section of the societies. She says, she is working on two of her novels which she is planning to publish in the coming years. She believes that writing is a freedom that one possesses, and writing not only helps in telling stories, but also helps in solving social issues predominantly existing in today's world.

Every Child lifeline /DEMO GOG international magazine

Free microphone

A magical tune.

It's great to dream alone
It takes time to understand yourself.
Quiet melodies from all over the world.
Let the ears of the heart be open to hear him.

The leaves of the trees dance in the wind,
And the water rushes from stone to stone,
Grasses caress each other.
The sun is watching from the sky.

Reeds are also special singers,
The whole existence gives pleasure if we understand it.
To understand this deeply.
We always need peace.

Even a leaf that falls to the ground.
If there is a slight breeze, it will scratch the ground.
And a wonderful melody is played, such a melody is created.

Each leaf is like a sheet of music,
Every piece of nature is a masterpiece.
Just to hear it...
Let the ears of our hearts be open.

Munavvar Boltayeva: Boltayeva Munavvar is 26 years old. Surkhandarya, Republic of Uzbekistan. His poems have been published in 5 poetry books, 7 international anthologies, America, Argentina, Egypt, Ecuador, Bulgaria, India, China, Great Britain, Indonesia, Colombia, Spain, Malaysia, Turkey, Korea, Singapore. International level volunteer. Participant of more than 90 International Conferences. Ambassador of more than 50 international level. "Poética Universal Filial Uzbekistan" Vice President. Winner of the "WIO GLOBAL WOMEN AWARD 2023" award. Ambassador of Wio Global Women Award Academy in Uzbekistan. Mighty Pens Award 2023 winner.

Smile...

I deleted the word sadness from my vocabulary.
I decorate the whole world with happiness.
To be a balm for a broken heart,
I encouraged everyone to laugh.

It's actually a joy to see every morning.
Even the chirping of a bird gives pleasure.
Hearts rejoice when looking around,
The waters sing like a song.

A smile is the beginning of happiness.
A smile means the end of sadness.
If you look in the mirror with a smile,
Know that your existence is a miracle, a fairy tale.

Life is beautiful because I am in it.
I smile at every test.
I know this morning is breaking for me.
I wish happiness to everyone.

My dears, always live happily.
Your existence is indeed a blessing.
Sing along and dance
Always smile and live in the palace of happiness.

Every Child lifeline /DEMO GOG international magazine

Free microphone

Руслан Саулебекович родился в 1977 году в Кармакшинском районе Кызылординской области Республики Казахстан. В 1996-2000 годах учился на факультете искусств Коркыт Атинского государственного университета. С 2001 года работает преподавателем Школы искусств Турымбета Салкинбаевича. Лауреат фестиваля работников образования «Наурыз шапагаты». Обладатель Гран-при конкурса «Гран-при года 2020» в Кыргызстане, диплом «Алтын калам» и медаль Чингиза Айтматова. Обладательница 1 места конкурса памяти поэтессы Гульсайры Момыновой, 2 места конкурса имени известного поэта Узбекистана Абдуллы Орипова. В районной газете «Кармакши таны» было опубликовано около 30 стихотворений. 8 стихотворений были опубликованы в литературном журнале «Пегас», где публиковались стихи поэтов из стран Средней Азии.

В ОСЕННЕМ САДУ

Дождливый день тоску наводит,
А ветер рвёт последний лист,
И мрачный день в раздумья клонит,
Туманный смог в окне завис.

Суров характер у природы,
Был сад в цвету – вновь листопад,
И пламя чувств в душе сегодня
Угаснет, как осенний сад.

В объятьях золотого сада
Хочу довериться душой,
С дождём мне выплакаться надо
Как небо, синею слезой.

И дождь без слов всё понимает,
Он спрячет горе в свой жилет,
Никто про слёзы не узнает,
Поэт и дождь – один секрет!..

ПОНЯТИЕ О ТРАДИЦИИ

"Чем иметь хорошие законы - имей хорошие традиции". (Народная мудрость) Традиции - это совокупность обычаев, образцы поведенческих типов в обществе, социальной группе, накопленные в течении веков согласно религии и составу народа. В повседневной жизни традиции являются качеством, отличающим различные культурные группы и неофициальным путём, регулирующим поведенческие правила и социальные деяния (Русско-казахский толковый словарь, ред, проф, Арын.Е, Павлодар, 2006). Традиции для нации являются жизненным кредо, устоявшимся законом общества, опытом духовной культуры, фундаментом обучения, воспитания и жизни. Во все времена требовалось неукоснительное исполнение требований и правил, заложенных в традициях, уважительное отношение к ним. Люди, нарушавшие эти незыблемые законы, всегда наказывались обществом. Традиции всегда были неотъемлемой частью жизни казахского социума. Например, свадьба, наурыз, проводы невесты, прием гостей, разделение радости, поздравления с новосельем - все это и многое другое отмечено в традициях предков. Традиции имеют большое познавательное, воспитательное значение. Исторически-социальные, бытовые, профессиональные аспекты жизни, поведенческие типы, педагогическое и духовное наследие - все осознается через традиции. Богатство традиций есть богатство культуры (Казахская энциклопедия, 7 том).

Жарас Кабишев родился 22.06.1970г. в Талдыкурганской области (ныне Жетысуйская), Булютобинском районе, в поселке Лепсы, на побережье озера Балхаш, на родине великого композитора Мукана Тулебаева.
Трудовую деятельность начал милиционером ППС в УВД Талдыкурганского облисполкома, затем сотрудником уголовного розыска.
В 1993 году продолжил работу в войсковой части 61812 на должности старшего разведчика.
С 2000 года по настоящее время работаю в охранной деятельности. писал стихи еще в школе,
занимается разъяснительной работой об обычаях и традициях казахского народа.
За активное участие в общественной деятельности в 2021г. был награжден медалью "Знак почета" в честь 155 летия Алихана Бокейханова.
За активное участие в общественной деятельности в 2023 году 14 июля награжден медалью "Патриот народа" решением комиссии общественных деятелей РК

Every Child lifeline / DEMO GOG international magazine

Free microphone

The Art of Teaching English:

A Pathway to Empowerment Introduction: Teaching English is a noble and rewarding profession that not only imparts language skills but also fosters personal growth and global communication. As the world becomes increasingly interconnected, the demand for English language proficiency has reached unprecedented heights.

This article aims to delve into the intricacies of teaching English, exploring various methodologies, techniques, and strategies that can empower both teachers and learners alike. 1. Understanding Language Acquisition: To effectively teach English, it is crucial to understand the process of language acquisition. Familiarity with theories such as behaviorism, cognitivism, and constructivism can help educators tailor their teaching methods to cater to individual learning styles. Recognizing that language learning goes beyond mere memorization but involves immersion, practice, and meaningful engagement is key. 2. Creating a Positive Learning Environment: Establishing a positive classroom environment is essential for effective teaching and learning. A warm and inclusive atmosphere encourages students to participate actively, take risks in language production, and develop their confidence gradually. Encouraging peer collaboration, providing constructive feedback, and celebrating successes foster an environment conducive to English language acquisition. 3. Utilizing Communicative Language Teaching (CLT): Communicative Language Teaching (CLT) emphasizes authentic communication as the primary goal of language learning. This approach emphasizes real-world situations where students engage in meaningful interactions using English as a medium of communication. Incorporating role-plays, debates, discussions, and problem-solving activities promote fluency while enhancing critical thinking skills. 4. Integrating Technology in Language Instruction: In today's digital age, technology has become an indispensable tool in teaching English effectively. Interactive whiteboards, online platforms for virtual classrooms or video conferencing provide endless opportunities for engaging learners in stimulating activities that enhance comprehension skills while fostering digital literacy. 5. Tailoring Lessons to Individual Learner Needs: Every student possesses unique strengths, weaknesses, and learning styles. Differentiating instruction to address these individual needs is essential. Employing varied teaching strategies, such as visual aids, hands-on activities, and audio recordings, ensures that students comprehend and retain the language more effectively. 6. Incorporating Culture into Language Teaching: Language and culture are intrinsically intertwined. Introducing cultural elements enhances language learning by providing context and encouraging a deeper understanding of linguistic nuances. By incorporating literature, music, films, or art from English-speaking countries into lessons, teachers can create more engaging and culturally enriching experiences for their students. 7. Continuous Professional Development: Teaching English is a dynamic field that necessitates continuous professional development to keep up with evolving methodologies and trends. Attending workshops, conferences, participating in online communities, and engaging in reflective practices ensures growth as an educator while equipping teachers with novel techniques to enhance their instructional strategies.

Conclusion: Teaching English is not merely about imparting grammar rules or vocabulary; it is about empowering learners to communicate effectively in an increasingly interconnected world. By understanding language acquisition processes, creating positive learning environments, incorporating communicative approaches, utilizing technology wisely, tailoring lessons to individual needs, integrating culture into language instruction, and embracing continuous professional development opportunities – educators can truly inspire students to become confident English speakers who can thrive in a global society.

Author: Makhfiratkhon Abdurakhmonova from Uzbekistan. Leader, Ambassador, Teacher, CEO of Leader Ladies Club organization, organizer of various projects.

Every Child lifeline /DEMO GOG international magazine

Free microphone

Dr. Ashok Chakravarthy Tholana is a writer, poet and reviewer, hailing from Hyderabad City, Telangana State, INDIA. His message-oriented poems on Universal Peace, World Brotherhood, Environment Consciousness, Protection of Nature, Safeguarding Children's and Human Rights have a rare distinction of getting published in no less than 90 countries. For his relentlessly contributions during the past 30-years, he has been conferred with several prestigious national and international awards, lots of laurels, commendations, titles etc. He also received applause from Dr. APJ Abdul Kalam, former-President, India, Shri Atal Behari Vajpayee, former-Prime Minister, India, Bill Clinton, USA, Queen Elizabeth of Britain, Princess of Wales, President and Prime Minister of France, Prime Minister of Switzerland, Senator Viktor Busa, The Lord President, Italy, United Nationals Organization, UNESCO, UNICEF etc.

Some Notable Awards / Honors include the **RABINDRANATH TAGORE LITERARY HONOR** jointly conferred by the Dept. of Culture, GOVT. OF SEYCHELLES & Motivational Strips, OMAN - Highest Honorary Title, **"GANDHIAN WORLD HARMONY CREATOR"** from Global Harmony Association, RUSSIA - **NAJI NAAMAN LITERARY PRIZE-2019**, LEBANON - Govt. of Gujarat, INDIA for **LITERARY EXCELLENCE** - H/E **YASSER ARAFAT PEACE AWARD-2019**, PEN International, PALESTINE - **GANDHIAN POET** - Global Harmony Association, RUSSIA - **WORLD POETIC STAR-2019 AWARD'**, KAZHAKSTAN - **EXCELLENCE IN WORLD LITERATURE** from WORLD LITERARY FORUM FOR PEACE AND HUMAN RIGHTS, NEPAL - **SWAMY VIVEKANANDA INTERNATIONAL PEACE AWARD' 2019** from the International Higher Academy Council Of English Literature (IHACEL-INDIA)

As of now, the poet has to his credit 10 published poetry volumes in English and 14 spiritual-oriented books translated from local Telugu language to English.

ETERNAL RADIANCE

Thoughts roam
In the fantasies room;
They keep whirling
To appease our longings.

Thoughts pluck the seeds
Treat mental peace as a weed,
Behind the screen of illusions
They knit a fabulous hallucination.

Thoughts often dissolve us
In a pre-fabricated bliss;
The day we cut its clutches
A new lease of life one fetches.

As the light of wisdom dawns
The light of knowledge crowns;
The darkness around gets dispelled,
An eternal radiance gets installed

SHARING JOYS

A global culture of peace
Should we cultivate in each,
Peace is a progressive option,
That removes all apprehensions.

Depicting a harmonious face,
Peace unifies the human race,
Why not we choose and desire,
To be tolerant and also to be fair.

The day peace adorns us
We are bound to feel real bliss,
Living for one another,
Is like sharing joys, forever.

Free microphone

Name : Niloy Rafiq Father : Mohammad Hossain Mother : Noorjahan Birth Place : Kalarmarchara, Moheshkhali, Cox's Bazar, Bangladesh. Date of Birth : 6th August, 1983 Mobile : +880 1816-026192 Email Id. : niloyrafiq@gmail.com The Number of published poetry (Number-7) : 1. Bishoddha Bishadey Bhashi Aami Raajhnash (I am the swan floating in the pure air)-2014 2. Pipasar Paramayu (Eternity of thirst)-2016 3. Nona Manusher Mukh (Salty human face)-2017 4. Aggato Agun (Unknown fire)-2019 5. Ankhi Anka Aadinath (Aadinath in eyes)-2021 6. Momer Prarthonay Noto Matir Shorir (Earthen body bended, worshipping candel)-2023 7. Sun Leaf (Rud Pata)-2023

Nice flight

Niloy Rafiq
Translated by Ashraful Kabir

On the north side of the island, I've to go to the march of the sun
I look at the roots, the memories are filled with tears
A familiar face is covered with cloud, a masked-face is eye-to-eye
Food warehouse is on fire! He did not come forward with his mouth open.

Burnt-wave pulls, midday meal with sister's artistry
Scenery at noon in the comfort of the earthen house, jingling anklets of peace
Poetic form is in the beautiful house of nature
Foggy-River cries! The sharp wink of the vulture.

In the bird's classroom, the engaged teacher of vocabulary
Is in the unity of melody, the man of the resounded treachery
Break the house for stealing down-under the river; blood-sucking coal lamentation!
No teenagers! Nice flight, the poet alone.

THE HEART CRIES
Niloy Rafiq

Pebbles in the cloud's door panel, flower in the secret eye
The boat of words beckons in the unknown sea
Forgetting the way, tossed on the river bank by waves,
A rain shower, a dumb face, the lost time.

The heart cries to see closely the river Bankkhali
A hazy mirror plays with beauty and warm love,
Soft smiling water lily with a yearning plea
Depressed is the tiller of the words of the root

Revolving by the nor'wester of divorced in summer
O the courageous sailor, have the patience of a craftsman
A gentle course against the current of the ebb tide
A great life expectancy in the city of nature.

Translated by Jyotirmoy Nandy

Every Child lifeline / DEMO GOG international magazine

Deborah Uzoma

AFRICA

Every Child lifeline /DEMO GOG international magazine

Face of the continent

A REPRESENTATION OF BAD FAITH IN ANDREW BULA'S THE SCHOOL CHAP: A NOVEL FOR YOUNGSTERS PRESENTED AT THE 5TH CHINUA ACHEBE INTERNATIONAL CONFERENCE @ INSTITUTE OF AFRICAN STUDIES, UNIVERSITY OF NIGERIA, NSUKKA IN COLLABORATION WITH PEARSON INSTITUTE FOR THE STUDY AND RESOLUTION OF CONFLICT ,UNIVERSITY OF CHICAGO, 22 JULY 2023.

BY UZOMA, DEBORAH CHINONYEREM

Abstract

This abstract explores the application of Jean-Paul Sartre's concept of bad faith in Andrew Bula's *The School Chap: A Novel for Youngsters*. The knowledge economy becomes increasingly important due to the rapid changes in an individual's transformational period. The narrative studies the story of a young protagonist navigating the challenges of school life and personal growth. Sartre's concept of bad faith, rooted in existentialist philosophy, provides a lens through which an analysis of the character's behavior and the implications of their actions. A close reading of the text is guided by the question: what constitutes bad faith in an individual's livelihood, its response to the real world, and the development of man? The essay investigates characters that experienced a state of bad faith. It reveals that bad faith occurs when characters engage in activities of self-deception, denying their freedom in expectations that hinder their genuine personal development. Additionally, it concludes that an individual who lives in bad faith suffers psychological guilt and that good faith can be achieved through sincerity.
Key concepts: Bad faith, good faith, children's literature, Existentialism

Introduction

Andrew Bula's *The School Chap: A Novel for Youngsters* constitutes a creative response to Jean-Paul Satre's concept of Bad Faith in Being and Nothingness, which according to Satre,(1943) Bad Faith is " a lie to oneself"(p.48). Jean-Paul Satre's concept of Bad Faith or "mauvaise foi", in French is a central idea in his existential philosophy. Satre is one of the fathers of existentialist theory. The existentialists believe that the human potential is defined as the capacity to experience one's freedom, so the ultimate existentialist would be someone who lives a life of freedom, or who maximizes his or her experiences (Taylor; 2006, p.216); although "by nature, human existence is subject to modification by forces outside itself" (Akwanya,2022, p. 37). This implies that while individuals have the capacity for freedom and self-determination, external factors can impact and shape their lives.

The lie is also a normal phenomenon of what Heidegger (1996), calls the "Mitsein"(p.49) Here, the essence of the lie implies that the liar is in complete possession of the truth which he is hiding. A man does not lie about what he is ignorant of; he does not lie when he spreads an error of which he is the dupe; he does not lie when he is mistaken. The ideal description of the liar would be a cynical conscious (Satre, 1943, p. 48). In other words, lies are a normal aspect of human social interactions, and the act of lying involves intentionally concealing the truth that the liar is aware of. It distinguishes lying from other forms of misinformation or unintentional errors.

Satre further posits that the liar intends to deceive. The only that changes everything is the fact that in bad faith, is that the liar hides the truth from himself. Satre argues that bad faith is a form of authenticity. Inauthenticity is the absence of authenticity which leads to a lack of positivity in human reality. In this state, individuals are not living in alignment with their authentic selves, and this can lead to a lack of positivity and fulfillment in their human reality. By adopting roles and denying one's self-realization, the person is termed to be living in bad faith. Bad faith is not infected or hereditary. It is a consciousness of the person itself. In bad faith, there is no preparation for the deceitful concept. But its very first act is to flee from the individual's responsibility, a disintegration from itself as to project what it cannot. "Bad faith flees being by taking refuge in "not-believing what one believes."(Satre, 1943, p.64). Sartre suggests that bad faith is a way for individuals to avoid confronting the existential reality of their existence and the freedom that accompanies it. It is a form of self-deception that allows individuals to

Deborah Uzoma is currently rounding off her Master of Arts in Literature at the University of Nigeria, Nsukka. She received a BA in English Studies at Imo State University, IMSU, Owerri. She writes essays, short stories, and plays. Her works have appeared in the Association of Nigerian Authors, Series, ANA, Everyline Life Magazine, Canada, and notable online journals. She is a performing poet and currently a freelance journalist with O town Media Gist and Entertainment blog where she documents campus chronicles and life events. Her writings have also won some notable awards which include, Brain Tracy Recognition,2021, Winner, Drama Workshop Point of Focus of the International Conference, Association of Nigerian Authors, ANA and AE-FUNAI, Ebonyi State, 2018, Young female writer of the month-January, Society for Young Nigerian Writers, January 2021, and a State Honours Award, NYSC Ebonyi State in 2017, among others. She can be reached at :uzomadeborah@gmail Com

Every Child lifeline /DEMO GOG international magazine
Free microphone

evade the authentic experience of being and the responsibility that comes with it. It has disarmed all beliefs in advance-those that it would like to take hold of and, by the same stroke, the others, those which it wishes to flee.

Strikingly, good faith can happen which is authentic existence. An important tenet of bad faith is that we must enact a bit of "good faith" to take advantage of our role to reach an authentic existence. Good faith wishes to flee the "not-believing-what-one-believes" by finding refuge in being. (Satre,19 49, p.69) The belief in being questions its identity. The appearance of belief according to Satre is a purely subjective determination without external correlation. (69).Sartre suggests that an important aspect of bad faith is the recognition that we need to embrace a certain amount of "good faith" in order to attain authenticity.

Good faith, in this context, refers to a genuine and sincere approach to life and existence. It involves a willingness to believe in and confront the truth of one's own beliefs, desires, and identity. The statement "not-believing-what-one-believes" of good faith is that while an individual undergoes bad faith, the individual tends to find refuge in genuine being, in truly acknowledging and embracing one's authentic self and existence. The novel also presents daily life experiences of people caused by them, and how they can navigate through those experiences. As a children's literature, there is evidence of the pupils who constitute characters in the novel struggle with conforming to prescribed gender roles and expectations influenced by their peers. Bula's narrative is set in Nigeria for school children (pupils). Again, there is a journey of self-discovery of personal identity -the tension between the protagonist, Kavnen, and other characters' desires and what they truly wanted to become which aligns with Satre's argument of bad faith. This research uses the qualitative method and adopts the existentialist theory. The interpretation of the novel is drawn from the lens of Jean-Paul Satre's concept of Bad Faith.

Analysis of Satre's Concept of Bad Faith in Bula's *The School Chap: A Novel For Youngsters*
The Lie
Sartre (1943), defines "Bad Faith," as "a lie to oneself and its goal is to put oneself out of reach" (p.48). This suggests a form of self-deception that is aimed at putting oneself out of reach of the uncomfortable aspects of one's existence. The individual apprehends the truth.

The novel revolves the brilliant, young school chap Kavnen who desires to be in school when his mate were, but the parents were unable to send him to school at an early age, unlike other Tiv Children. In the novel, he is described as "the most creative of them"(p.2) When he is eventually enrolled in school by his mother, he tells lies to his mother that he has no rival in his class. He receives much attention from his classmates and feels that no one is like him in the class, so "Kavnen became proud"(The School Chap:2021,p.47). Unfortunately, he loses the first position to Mnena, his rival "By this time, the headmaster was saying his own name as the pupil who took the second position in the class. Kavnen bowed his head and tears flowed freely from his eyes as he moved to the front of the assembly to be recognized" (p.50-52) . With this announcement, Kavnen is saddened by this outcome.

Lying is a negative attitude. The liar is in complete possession of the truth that he is hiding (Satre, 1943, p.48). This suggests that an individual who lies does not lie about what he is ignorant of, either a mistake, rather the individual who lies denies a conscious truth. The excerpt reveals Kaven telling lies to his mother "She had asked Kavnen one day if he had a rival in his class. But Kavnen had confidently replied that he had none. In fact, he had even boasted that he would surely have the best result in his class"(P.47). Kaven ponders over his loss, the disappointment from his mother and the fact that she would "never fulfill her promise to him, except he took the first position in the examination results of his class"(p.52) Kavnen gets a rubber ring from a Magician to make him the best in his class. "Then Kavnen thought he was armed to take revenge against Mnena by becoming the pupil with the best result in class in the second term" (p.58) Even this proves abortive and by the end of the term, he loses to Mnena again (p.61). Kavnen hides the truth that his educational success lies in studying and not in the magician rubber. Satre argues that Bad faith refers to self-deception and dishonesty individuals engage in to evade their roles and responsibilities. Bad faith has in appearance the structure of falsehood.

Adding to our discussion, we see that the rich parent's neighbor isolates Kavnen because of his poor background but because their children cannot sing some Tiv songs, this allows Kavnen to have a brief interaction with them: "so whenever the children met to play, Kavnen taught them many games. There was one game that he taught them that the children particularly liked. It was, in fact, the song in it that drove them crazy, playful, and free".

(P.2) On one occasion, Kavnen receives a beating from one of their rich neighbour's mother for peeping through the window to watch television despite being warned severally. This, in turn, affects his eyes, as "there was only a discoloration on the sclera part of it". According to Satre's argument, Bad faith requires that I should not be what I am: that is that there is an imponderable difference separating being from nonbeing in the mode of being of human reality. (p.66). This suggests that Sartre believes that there is a fundamental distinction between existence (being) and non-existence (non-being) within the realm of human reality. Kavnen fails to acknowledge this distinction and instead chooses to deny or ignore their existence-the difference between the rich and the poor choice.

Faith is Faith
Satre(1943), avers that the true problem of bad faith "stems evidently from the fact that bad faith is faith" (p.65). Sartre argues that the true problem of bad faith arises from the fact that bad faith is still a form of faith. Despite its deceptive nature, bad faith involves a kind of belief or acceptance of something. It suggests that individuals who engage in bad faith are not completely devoid of faith but rather have a distorted or misguided form of it.

In the text, the pupils of Firm Foundation fell into bad faith at the hand of the school bully, Ashi. Ashi is described thus :The name of the girl was Ashi, and she was in the habit of always threatening younger pupils to give her some of their food or she would beat them up. Those who did were spared. But those who did not were hurt. Worse still, her victims feared that if they reported her, they would see the worst of her just as she warned it would happen. Many pupils were afraid of her. So, it seemed as if Ashi was above the law. (P.30)The above depicts the state of the pupils of Firm Foundation inflicted by Asher. Kavnen challenges the school bully, Ashi. Kavenen reveals his might and thus, gains freedom not for himself alone but for other pupils in bad faith. "And from that day onwards, the aggressive girl became quiet and withdrawn. All the pupils once afraid of Ashi now went about their days without the slightest fear of being bullied"(32). This act of Kavnen aligns with Satre's (1943) statement that a person frees himself by the very act by which he makes himself an object for himself (p. 65). This suggests an awareness of oneself and self-reflection, a person can potentially gain a sense of freedom from external influences, societal expectations, and even preconceived notions.

Kavnen's father, Kungwa, puts himself

Free microphone

out of reach and this is an escape and goal of bad faith. Kungwa, a driver in a private hospital is described in the novel as "irresponsible" (The School Chap,2021, p.1). Most of his salary goes on drinking and womanising and only a little goes on just feeding his family. And so even at the age of eight, Kavnen had never been to school. Isese, his older sister by two years, had never been to school too" (The School Chap, 2021, p .1). In the words of Satre(1943) "Bad faith does not hold the norms and criteria of truth as they are accepted by the critical thought faith"(p.68) portrays Sartre's view that bad faith involves a distorted form of faith, deviating from the accepted norms and criteria of truth. Kungwa depicts this mode of thinking and being that objectifies truth and misrepresents the nature of being (his true self and taking up his fatherly responsibilities). The authentic domain of bad faith is realizing that the role we are playing is a lie. As the narrative unfolds, Kungwa victimizes himself. His attitude causes him to fear the future.

In the novel, Kungwa is sad because he sees that his position as the head of his family is not in place. Secondly, the children give Tabitha, his wife, so much attention and just give him a little (The School Chap p.15). This brooding eventually results to a fight between him and Tabitha. Kungwa beats her: Tabi!' he shouted a short form of his wife's name. 'Today, you will tell me why you sent my children to school without telling me,' Kungwa announced, as he drew out a brown leather belt from his trousers and angrily advanced towards her (p.40) And in turn, Tabitha abuses him "Stupid man! Why should I tell you? ... Why should I tell you? Womanizer! Why should I tell you? Shouldn't you be the one to send your children to school? Do you care? Are you a man? Leave me alone! Drunk!" (42), this results to a state of disharmony in the family.

Another character is Tabitha, the mother of Kungwa who in the novel depicts an industrious woman despite the harsh condition she encounters - "a woman who barely enjoyed the sweetness of her husband, she always found ways of meeting her needs"(The School Chap, 2021 p.7). Tabitha seeks ways to enroll her two children in school by farming and selling the products afterward. "One such way was in cultivating a yam farm on the outskirts of Gamkiki many years ago. It was a small-scale farm, just enough to feed and sell off a few yam tubers to meet simple pressingNeeds (P.7) Again, in bad faith, a certain version of truth emerges, along with a particular mode of thinking and a specific way of being that resembles that of objects. Again, owing to the injury Kavnen sustains on his eyes from their rich neighbors, Tabitha is " deeply saddened. And she reasoned that if she tried her best and sent her son to school, in the future Kavnen could buy himself a TV and a DVD player. The individuals in bad faith treat truth as an object, something external and fixed, rather than as a dynamic and subjective concept. A person can live in bad faith which does not mean that he does not have an abrupt awakening to cynicism or good faith but that which requires a consistent and particular style of life. (Satre, 1949, p.50). This suggests that a person can live in a state of bad faith, which means they are engaging in self-deception or denial of their true beliefs and desires. So, Tabitha does this to win the Children's love and they give her all attention.

Good Faith

Good faith embraces genuine belief and finds refuge in being, while bad faith involves self-deception and avoidance of authentic beliefs through not believing what one truly believes. It is a turning point where a person recognizes the significance of living by their true self and principles.

Significantly, Kavnen tries again. He realizes himself and studies hard this time. On the contrary, Mnena becomes "a bit proud, outspoken" and expects to be the "highest performer in Primary 1 A again. Besides, she now had many friends and had equally become well-known"(p.66). Unfortunately for her, Kavnen emerges first in his class. "Kavnen came first in Primary 1 A. He was so excited because his dream had finally come true. (p. 67) Moreso, Mnena receives a prize too but for Kavnen, "Dr. Adezua gave a big TV to Kavnen and an extra prize of a DVD player. Even, the proprietor promised that if Kavnen continued to do well as he had done, he would sponsor him through secondary school and up to the university level" (68). Kavnen becomes an owner of a big TV and a DVD player for which his eyes then were attacked by a rich neighbor because Kaven's family had none(6). Jean-Paul Sartre (1943) posits that, "being is full positivity. It knows no otherness. It never posits itself as other than another being. It can support no connection with the other. It is self indefinitely and it exhausts itself in being" (62). According to Sartre, "being" is characterized by full positivity". This suggests that existence, in its essence, is a state of complete affirmation or affirmation of itself. It does not recognize or acknowledge any form of otherness or external identity.

Kavnen's engagement in his true self brings him to the limelight and thus a re-affirmation of his being, even before enrolling in school, his brilliance is not disputed. It is also at this point that Tabitha resolves to fulfill her promise again "She was satisfied. 'Thank you so much for making me proud, my son', she later told Kavnen. 'I shall now fulfill my promise to you, she added, her face beaming with satisfaction (p.67).

As the story progresses, Tabitha apologizes to his Kungwa, and their family peace and harmony are restored "Soon after the apology, Kungwa smiled, saying that he had forgiven her. Kavnen became very happy to see his parents at peace with each other"(P.45). An abrupt awakening to good faith suggests a sudden realization of the importance and value of authenticity, sincerity, and genuine belief.

Guilt:

From the explication of the characters, we see that the characters suffer a bit of guilt in their actions. Grene (1951) and Sartre (1943) challenge the everyday understanding of guilt as merely breaking moral requirements, being punishable, having debts, or having responsibilities.

In the context of Sartre's philosophy, psychological guilt is associated with the conduct of bad faith. It involves not accepting one's responsibilities as a conscious and free individual (For-itself), and instead seeking to blame others or external factors for one's actions. It also entails selectively asserting one's freedom when it serves one's interests while resorting to a theory of psychological determinism at other times. Grene, refers to the consciousness of doing a wrong that could have been avoided and for which one is personally responsible.((Greene, 1951, pp. 166-17). For Heidegger, "guilt is in a sense of "breaking a moral requirement," or "making oneself punishable," or "having debts" or "having responsibility" necessarily defined as a lack" (pp. 260-261). Heidegger's assertion implies that guilt is necessarily not an inherent quality or characteristic, but rather emerges as a result of a deficiency or shortfall in meeting moral requirements or responsibilities.

Conclusion

Satre's concept of bad faith is in an age-appropriate manner. It confronts the opposing tendencies of good faith and bad faith. It provides valuable lessons on embracing freedom, taking responsibility, and living authentically. It also summarises the dangers of self-deception and the importance of embracing one's freedom and taking responsibility for any choices.

From the exploration of some characters in the novel, it challenges the reader to always question some societal expecta-

Every Child lifeline /DEMO GOG international magazine

Free microphone

tions and predefined roles, such as Tabitha is seen taking up both the fatherly and motherly responsibility at some point. We see a revelation of predefined roles as Kungwa realizes himself and turns on a new leave. His son, Kavnen navigates through the journey of school life and personal growth. Similarly, Heidegger comments that "human realities" must be a relation of being and this relation must cause "human realities" to depend on one another in their essential being" (quoted in Being 244). In this view, human reality cannot exist without a relationship with the other in its existence. It is this other that proves human existence as a journey of inauthentic or authentic.

However, Bula's *The School Chap: A Novel for Youngsters* made the short list of the Association of Nigerian Authors, ANA 2022 prize for Children's literature. The novel has also been recommended for reading in JSS1 all over Nigeria by NERDC and made a complementary textbook and instructional materials for use in FCT Education Resource Centre from August 2022 - July 2025. Additionally, Bula is also a novelist, poet, poetry performer, film actor, and essayist, whose critical works have been published in Nigeria, London, and other parts of the country.

References

Akwanya, Amechi Nicholas. (2013). "Angst in Rainer Maria Rilke's Duino Elegies." *Journal of Humanities and Social Science* 13. 6: 37. Google Book Search. 15March 2022.

Bula, Andrew. (2021). *The School Chap: A Novel for Youngsters*. Mindfield publishing.

Carman, Taylor. (2006). "The Concept of Authenticity." *A Companion to Phenomenology and Existentialism*. eds. Hubert L. Dreyfus and Mark A. Wrathall. Oxford Blackwell.

Grene, Marjorie (1951). "Authenticity: An Existential Virtue." *Ethics*, vol. LXII, pp. 166-17.

Heidegger, Martin. (1996). Being and Time. Trans. Joan Stambaugh. State U of NY.
Sartre, Jean-Paul. (1943). Being and Nothingness. London, Routledge.

Bio: Deborah Uzoma is currently rounding off her Master of Arts in Literature at the University of Nigeria, Nsukka. She received BA in English Studies at Imo State University, IMSU, Owerri. She writes essays, short stories, and plays. Her works have appeared in the Association of Nigerian Authors, Series, ANA, Everyline Life Magazine, Canada, and notable online journals. She is a performing poet and a freelance journalist with O town Media Gist and Entertainment blog where she documents campus chronicles and life events. Her writings have also won some notable awards which include, Brain Tracy Recognition, 2021, Winner, Drama workshop point of Focus of the International Conference, Association of Nigerian Authors, ANA and AE-FUNAI, Ebonyi State, 2018, Young female writer of the month-January, Society for Young Nigerian Writers, January 2021 among others.

Email : deborah.uzoma.90728@unn.edu.ng
Facebook: https://www.facebook.com/deborahuzoma
Linkedin: https://www.linkedin.com/in/deborah-uzoma-82235815a
+2347066186843

WAKE UP COUNTRY MEN

*Wake up country men, wake up
on a keg of gunpower we sit,
daily weeping as we grieve
The drums of battle drumming
harder, louder, and clearer
fire of destruction blowing all around.
Hand of war extending here and there,
grip of fear quaking all and sundry
as in this country we hunger and mourn.*

*Wake up country men, wake up
Bloodshed and uncertainty greet
Us squarely daily to our faces,
as we are runned down, down and down
Corruption and lies drink up our glory*

*Wake up country men, wake up
bury corruption to its lasting grave.
Stuff your mouth with truth
that shines via via via like the stars
Wear transparency as a sailing guide,
and naked truth as our meal,
To build, not to looth, our obvious task
Since the drill of million holes in our economy
dries us up like dry leaves in its season
Let's wash off grab it all syndrome,
Wash off ethnicism, partisan politics,
Wash off over zealous religion and nepotism
So we can up-root those
Who dries us in the dry cleaners*

*Then our country can stand tall again
And flag the deep green Olive branch in gain
Can we answer this Clarion call?
Who should take the lead?
The die is cast,
The cast is vast
And the vast we must cover fast.*

Lolo Tessyfrancis Ofoegbu.
A poet, Vice Chairman ANA IMO.

Every Child lifeline /DEMO GOG international magazine

Free microphone

Born as Ibrahim Yusuf Ibrahim, also known as I. Y. I. He held from Nigeria and writes at leisure from the comfort of his bed. Contact at: iyifagge20021991@gmail.com

TO YOU I SURRENDER

Time without number
More than I can remember
I wont stop nor slumber
You make me to fonder
To you I surrender
To caress not to plunder

SERENITY

My hope in adversity
Am loving you till infinity
Ever lasting to eternity
Stronger than the trinity
In accordance to morality
Pure intention and sincerity
With you am in serenity

Mourn/Forget the Mortal World

& the sky wears a face
of what we are still looking for,
some days we mourn/forget
the world where people disappear
without dying.

How I wish
but here wishes are our broken wings,
before then
we could measure & dig our grave
beneath the sand & stones &
rename ourselves
now everyone carries a grave in his body
a dogged shadow, a red flag
for death is delaying.

Some days
even the familiar sky
wears its face outside out
without a torment gawn;
the only ammunition that can kill
with bullet of our sins/fears
there are duvet witted with our
mourning/prayers
& the sorrows that hawked on
the wall
of our diminishing
I'm not denying this gradual dying.

Usaini Abubakar (Alhussain) is a Nigerian poet who hails from Jos, Plateau State, Nigeria. He is a motivational script writer, bibliophile, an introvert and a well-trained teacher. Usaini has been meritoriously awarded many certificates for his literary achievements. He also contributes frequently to "World Voice Magazine".

Every Child lifeline /DEMO GOG international magazine

Free microphone

GOODBYE, MOTHER EARTH

The earth is squeezing her breasts.
But her milk is falling on empty lips.
Siblings are chewing deadly sorrow,
Yet typhoid and malaria are their friends.
The earth is like a radio
Listening to our yesteryear tears.
All hail! Saturated toothpicks,
Golden is your spherical shape.
Goodbye, Mother Earth.
I'm just a visitor standing at your gate.
Once I am called in by Mr. Rabbit,
I'll leave you with a sorrowful goodbye.
Do you want to know my name?
Do you want to be my best friend?
Follow not the taste of my appetite;
I can whisper at any moment.
O mother earth,
Don't spoil your tears for my sake.
Even if I am welcomed in happily,
Never again will we converse like before.

©Gabriel S. Weah

Who Will Cry For My Corpse?

O dear God, maker of the globe,
Hear me now; I'm greeted with tears.
The ravens have eaten my nostrils.
And the emptiness of life has dowried me.
With my voice, I screamed loudly,
Yet my dearest breath is now creeping.
If I fall without touching success,
Take my corpse and offer me a prayer.
Who shall cry for my corpse?
My ribs have rejected my body.
And tears eloquently laughing.
But if pain consumes me, do not laugh!
O life, why hast thou forsaken me?
The ants and rats are eating from my bowl.
Yet you're nourishing my head with pain.
Who shall cry for my corpse?
Your tasty seasons are given to the dogs.
And all you tell me is to have patience.
Can't you see how thirsty I am?
O life, when shall my lips appraise you?
 Goodbye, salty earth,
It wasn't my plan to leave you in tears.
Brokenhearted is my burning lips.
I am gone; one day, we shall see again.

©Gabriel S. Weah

Poet, essayist, life coach and mentor, teacher (by profession), and devout Christian, Gabriel S. Weah, alias "Lyrical Genius," is an eminently multi-talented Liberian award-winning poet who learned his writing career in a dream.

Every Child lifeline /DEMO GOG international magazine

Free microphone

STILL I RISE
Thrown overboard into the Atlantic
Meal for the aquatic
A buoy; still I rise.

Ripped from solace
Cast into furnace
A gold; still I rise.

Stripped of ego
To hide like gecko
A star; still I rise.

Flushed down history
To wallow in misery
A diamond; still I rise.

Grinded to dust
Left to rust
A pyramid; still I rise.

Thrown into flame
To be consumed by shame
A phoenix; still I rise.

Cut to pieces
Never to find where peace is
A hydra; still I rise.

Born of resilience
Nurtured by pestilence
An African; still I rise.

PILGRIMS
In all the religions
Of the different earth regions
Always, all we men
Have been pilgrims of women.

Francis Otole is a Nigerian born poet and academician. A member of the Association of Nigerian authors (ANA) and many other literary groups. He is an award winning poet from the local and international scenes. Has been featured in magazines, journals, and anthologies; locally and internationally. He is a graduate of the prestigious Benue State University and a student of life. His hobby is reading and writing. He is married with two children.

Every Child lifeline /DEMO GOG international magazine

The relationship between symbol and belief in the plastic arts

What distinguishes a person is his physical expression of his feelings, which is considered one of the practical and spiritual needs

And since the popular arts and their history are considered linked to the originality and life of peoples and artists in particular, the symbol is considered the expression of those temporal and historical connotations, to get to know those arts through them.

If form and content are an organic composition left by art, in its thinking and consciousness, motivated by feeling and the stimulus to creativity as a result of coexistence, deepening and suffering of experience, and coming out with the form of experience with a degree of reconciliation, as long as that creativity belongs to an era, time and society of the artist.

The symbol, technically the object of our neutrality, is the distinctive language, expressing a particular society with all its unique cultural values of the people who gave birth

to it, expressing its soil throughout history, its extent of its ancient heritage and the reflection of those characteristics on the content in the form of available tools and means of expression.

All this is a real translation of the language used by the people's artist to express his feelings and the feelings of his society, including events, beliefs and ideas.

The work of art is not a record of fact but a form of expression.

But the fact that a work of art does not register reality does not mean that it is distant from it, as is the case with practical symbols.

The work of art in this way is not reality in its form, but reality in its general form which knows no time or place.

And if art, in this sense, is tangible, abstract, then science is also a symbol of abstract convention, but the difference between abstraction in the two cases is clear from the fact that the scientist in the course of his work does not deal with tangible reality, if not with what he observes from certain phenomena in it, then he takes these specific phenomena and tries to apply them in many situations and fields through some special conventional symbols, and the resulting values \u200b\u200bare abstract values that are far from tangible reality.

The artist is often an individual sensitive to his surroundings and is influenced by the different chromatic values, the relationship of forms to each other, the reverberation of sounds, their tonality, the texture of things and their differences, and is rarely concerned with the value of his surroundings from a utilitarian or material point of view.

In the end something different from reality comes out, but it is related to it, the artistic symbols are not reality, but at the same time they are related to it, they are abstract

Art is more real than reality.

This on the one hand, and on the other hand, we see that the fact that the works of art are sensory symbols, abstract, makes them more real than the tangible reality, and if it objectively represents the truth, then from the subjective side it only represents parts of it, and perhaps the part does not represent the whole, nor does the particular express the general, then the work of art is more real than the tangible reality, as it includes many meanings while its forms are easy.

Abstract look:

It all depends on the visual registration of the print, and the artist may start with natural forms, but they are soon gradually stripped away to become lines and shapes that have relationships that follow each other, yet far from apparent

Every Child lifeline / DEMO GOG international magazine

nature.

The abstract is an attempt to summarize and reveal the laws of form with as few lines and shapes as possible, as we find in the works of the ancients, where hieroglyphics such as family, water, the key of life and the falcon have been stripped, and shows how the Egyptian extracted these shapes from nature and placed them in new areas of writing to give new meanings.

Similarly, in Coptic art, they used the head of a lioness and a human body to express the war machine. The fish, cross, dove, sheep, eagle, sword and key were all used to express specific meanings. Similarly, the Islamic artist in his engineering works and his repetitive plant paintings, abstracted from nature and his writings that superimposed decoration as an important aspect in artistic construction. The space is based on the fact that it can carry meanings, just like musical melodies do, love feelings without relying on external natural origin, and these meanings are still widespread up to our present era, so the dove symbolizes peace, and the eagle symbolizes strength, and the symbolism is similar in terms of evoking some meanings to the shorthand process in writing.

Code features:

Due to the importance of the symbol, it is necessary to recognize its artistic and social characteristics, characteristics and values, as symbolism has many meanings: it can mean the expression of a distinct idea or a recording of realistic facts in an abstract form.

Art code:

It is the unit, or decorative form, which is used and inspired by the environment and on the basis of which the artistic work produced by the People's Artist is based, so that its production obtains a distinctive and unique character expressing the qualities and values expressing the beliefs, traditions and culture of its environment, which includes the floor with which all human beings interact. of plastic language, simple processing, simplicity and his ability to express himself motivated by reaching his needs through the resulting form without obstacles and without borders, reaching the summit of individuality, in the art where his beliefs, traditions and the extension of his faith in it.

The People's Artist has been given birth to a spirit of freedom, which makes him express his status and personality beyond the limit of his beautification instinct in his works, preserving his emotional and related history with the inherited traditions and customs of his society, expressing them in his various arts and crafts, emphasizing his fantasies and perceptions of life outside and inside himself. Between two different worlds, the human and animal world, or the human and elven world. The clothes take the shape of the veil in triangles of different sizes, with their geometric shapes as well as the rectangle, the rhombus, and the point, or their use of metal buttons that are added in the shape of a ring, as well as the longitudinal or transverse lines. The dot expresses the sting and the line on the waist, and the triangle represents the veil that contains evil within it, protecting the soul by wearing this dress, the diamond, the square and the circle, and repeating it five times to express five and five, as it performs the function of the palm (hand) to ward off evil.

Bedouin Tattoo Symbols And Their Social Meaning And History:

What the tattoo symbols with which the Bedouins mark their camels, horses and other possessions deserve is to have the same tattoo inscriptions with which they mark certain subjects of their body for their interest in the customs and traditions of the manual arts and for their social and historical significance for them.

Tattoo symbols vary according to the tribes, bellies and other Bedouin groups that use them as a distinctive emblem. Some of them are made up of simple units such as vertical or horizontal lines, leaning to the right or left, arrows, circles, triangles or crosses, and some are made up of complex shapes of two or more similar or different units, or other more complex shapes.

The Bedouins call each of these units by a special name, expressing the things they symbolize, or the places that tattoo their symbols. The symbols adopted by Eastern Bedouins in Sinai and Northern Red Sea Governorate differ from those adopted by Western Bedouins in Matrouh and New Valley Governorates, and by Southern Bedouins in Aswan and Southern Sea Governorates. And the tribe itself, regardless of its stomach, is enough to adopt a unified symbol without the use of additional symbols at the end.

Souad Khalil

Every Child lifeline /DEMO GOG international magazine

Face of the continent

Tanja Ajtic was born in Belgrade, Serbia. She lived and studied in Serbia at the Faculty of Philology-Department of Serbian Language and Literature. Since 2002, she lives and creates in Canada, Vancouver. Moved to Belgrade, Serbia in summer 2023. She is a member of many groups and associations. Her poems and stories have been published two hundred collections (books), anthologies, electronic books and magazines. Her poems have been published in English, Serbian, Chinese, Croatian, Iraqi, Bengali, Indian, Bulgarian, Tunisian, Arabic. In the spring of 2018, at the "Pegasus" competition of the Literary Youth of Serbia, Belgrade, she won the award for printing the first book of poetry "Outlines of Love". Her book was exhibited at the Book Fair in 2018 in Belgrade, as well as at the Book Salon in Toronto in 2019. She is represented in the Anthology among the 30 best writers for 2020 by the Association of Writers of Australia. She won first place, the award of authors from abroad in the Federation of BiH (2020) and the second prize in Great Britain from the Serbian Library in London. Participated in book fairs with collections and anthologies with other authors. Won III World Prize for Excellence "Cesar Vallejo" 2021 in the category of artistic excellence, Peru, by the World Spanish Union of Writers and International Award of Excellence, "Cita Del Galateo" Antonio De Ferrariis, IX edition 2022 – Rome, Italy, prestigious prize for a group of poets in the English language; winners of Foundation Naji Naaman literary prize 2023; winning the 2023 "Zheng Nian Cup" Literary Award – Third Prize by the Beijing Mindfulness Literature Museum. She is the winner of many awards, diplomas and certificate. She is currently writing poetry, short stories, haiku, gogyoshi poetry as well as graphics artist as a freelance artist. Hers art graphic were published in books and magazines.

A River

You who live near the river
You believe in images of little gods of love
in ancient Roman art
and Renaissance as well as a new era.
In a lovely little winged child entertained with
various jobs
you see them and speak like Socrates:
"I know I do not know anything!"
You say that the world is a property without a master
and that it is not known who its creator is?
You as a free thinker, neither good nor bad,
indifferent, but not powerless.
You see those beautiful children in the glare of the river
which flows for you into infinity and you enjoy.
You have a safe haven and enough air
to survive everything
in the air that can cause it
chemical changes and you can calculate them
only if you want.
You live in your own reflection of an image
and I believe you
that the world can be a nice place
if we look at ourselves.
Then everything is clear.

Eternal curse

We like to emphasize splendor, significance, reputation and fame
rather than modesty, contrition and true love.
We want to give one thing a relief that catches the eye,
to be particulary emphasized.
And if we have relief maps, we don't know how to measure.
We wander and saunter at night.
At night without dreams.
We postpone forgiveness and omissions.
We are postponing our payment deadline,
we also want to have a discount while we are paying,
and we would like to do everything to make it cheaper.
And paradise is not bought but deserved.

If we return everything we took
and wish forgiveness of sins, mercy and forgiveness,
to be forgiven we will feel the same.
After the main flowering, the flowers will bloom once again.

And we will survive.
Like being born again
the revival of classical antiquity
or more precisely freedom
and the creative human spirit under the influence of classical
literature,
of art and philosophy in the Renaissance.

We will renew our lives
and fix and change it for the better.
We will refresh and rejuvenate.
We will look at hummingbirds that have bigger brain
in relation to the body of other birds.
Heart too.
These birds can fly
in all directions, as they please!
They can live for a long time by feeding on
flower nectar and candied water.
We, like them, are small but a lot is expected of us.

Rejection and refusal,
as a musical repetition of the same tone, the
opposite is an echo.
Everything will resonate.

Rejection and refusal happen to us
like breaks in a circus that clowns fill with their jokes.
We avoid the eternal curse
because there is always hope for a corrective exam
and a place under the sun for us.
We can be dignified,
be those who produce again,
which recreate.
We can multiply and experience
content to revive consciousness,
get a good voice again
for the person and respect, reputation and name.

It is never too late for natural things
to make us feel better.
It's all in us
in our big hearts in the body of a small hummingbird.
We have everything you need!
Naturally!

Every Child lifeline /DEMO GOG international magazine

10th Americas Poetry Festival of New York

My different impression at The 10th Americas Poetry Festival of New York 2023
(By Kieu Bich Hau – Vietnamese author)

Most of the time, I only need to be patient, still and wait for my opportunities while I continue to work hard everyday for my target, the the mystical will come to me suddenly. That is my experience I have achieved on the way to the poetry land and on my literary journey of over 30 years of my life. It was really a miracle to me when I was the first Vietnamese author in its history to be the invitee of The 10th Americas Poetry Festival of New York 2023.

<u>Writer – the most expensive job</u>

When I was a child, I had a specific image of America, as a promised land, a dream for people with talent and new ideas. No matter how crazy your ideas are, but if they can bring benefits to the people, yourself and the community, contributing to improving society, they are all accepted and honored, regardless of your background or what country you come from...

I consider myself a different person, my brain always comes up with strange ideas, which if told to children, they consider it a fairy tale, and if shared with adults, they laugh. I am a crazy person, I am the only one who believes that what I see will soon become a reality and will help humanity. Those are the reasons which lead me dreaming that one day I will go to America and express myself there.

And then that miracle came when a mentor appeared, who was strong enough, convincing enough to make me understand that I am born for poetry, for literature, the tragedy of this life of mine is the driving force for me to step into a new area of light - poetry. I wrote poetry and sent my poems to the world, with the desire to express my love, share my discoveries on my journey of self-healing, and have found a poetic path, healing division and conflict in all circumstances. Love, Light, Poetic Journey, and the art of living wisely are the main topics for my poetry to express. I have sent my poems to the literary magazines, platforms, and poetry events across many countries where I have fellow poets. And then my poems, although simple, but filled with love and whispers about how to soothe yourself, soothe the world, open wide arms to friends around the world, have found sympathy and spread radiately. Thanks to that, I continuously received invitations to participate in the different Poetry Festivals and literary forums in Asia and Europe. At this point, having been awakened and clearly aware of my literary mission, I did not save or procrastinate my dream anymore, I gave top priority to my participation in world literary events, connecting with literary friends in beautiful, intense emotions. I accepted to pay high prices for long literary trips, accepting that I might lose my job when I returned back my home country. Just as author Ocean Vuong said, writing is the most expensive profession! How many famous authors in the world of literature have spent their entire lives in poverty, with proud hearts, exhausting themselves for their works!

My poetic trip in New York

In early August 2023, I was surprised to receive an invitation from the Organizing Committee of the 10th Americas Poetry Festival of New York, taking place in New York (USA). This is a multilingual poetry event, taking place in the 1st half

Every Child lifeline /DEMO GOG international magazine

10th Americas Poetry Festival of New York

of October every year. This year's event took place from October 11-13, 2023. The Americas Poetry Festival of New York is organized by the College of Interdisciplinary Arts and Sciences of the City University of New York in collaboration with the Walt Whitman Birthplace Association and the Cervantes Institute of New York. The event's steering committee includes American professors and poets: Carlos Aguasaco, Yrene Santos, and Carlos Velásquez Torres.

About the three curators of the Americas Poetry Festival of New York, I only got to know poet Carlos Velásquez Torres in May 2023, when we were both invited to the 13th Europa in Versi (The Poetry Festival) in Como (Italy). While attending the poetry event in Italy, Mr. Carlos Velásquez Torres and I talked often, from the time we were picked up at the airport, to the intensive poetry reading sessions, or during our walks to explore the old squares in Como. Poet Carlos Velásquez Torres is a lively, funny, chatty and warm person, the true Latin American personality.

He was born in Colombia, but immigrated to the United States over the past two decades, currently teaching at the City University of New York and being an editor of the publishing house Artepoética Press in New York. After the event in Como, we returned our home countries and continued to keep in touch. After that, he organized the publication of my poetry collection "Two Moons" (English version) by the Artepoética Press. But I still did not know that he was one of three important curators in the Organizing Committee of the Americas Poetry Festival of New York, until the day I suddenly received an invitation to participate in this important event. It was truly a dream, the most wonderful thing that I was lucky enough to have when I decided to commit and bet the rest of my life on literature and mysterious poetry trips.

Welcoming me at the JFK airport (New York) were three people: Professor Carlos Aguasaco, Dean of the College of Interdisciplinary Arts and Sciences of the City University of New York and Head of the Organizing Committee of the Americas Poetry Festival of New York, poet Carlos Velásquez Torres and Guatemalan poet: Miguel Angel Oxlaj Cusmez. On the way from the JFK airport to the Chelsea Savoy Hotel where foreign poets stayed, poet Carlos Velásquez Torres drove, while professor Carlos Aguasaco took the opportunity to interview me about Vietnam, Hanoi, and introduce important buildings, landscapes, and points of New York along the way. He also asked about the price of a can of Coca Cola in Hanoi (0.4 cents), and was surprised when compared to the price of 5 USD for it in New York. He also said that the rent fee for a small studio apartment in New York was up to 5,000 USD/month. Indeed, it is extremely expensive in New York.

The 10th Americas Poetry Festival of New York had 31 participating authors, including 20 American authors and 11 foreign authors (India, Spain, Romania, Ireland, Colombia, Mexico, Argentina, Nepal, Peru, Vietnam, Guatemala). Professor Carlos Aguasaco said that, during the 10 times of the Americas Poetry Festival, the Organizing Committee has welcomed more than 300 authors to attend the event and present their works, besides American poets, they have also welcomed other authors from more than 60 countries. In 2023, for the first time, the Organizing Committee invited an author from Vietnam. From Asia, there have been Japanese, Korean, and Chinese authors attending this event in previous years.

In the morning of October 11, 2023, I arrived in New York and the Opening Ceremony of the Poetry Festival took place in the evening. There were 16 poets reading their poems in the Opening Ceremony, including me. I had prepared two poems in advance to read bilingually in Vietnamese and English at the Opening Ceremony, which are "The anger" and "How to hold this longing?" Due to the big traffic jam in New York, the Organizing Committee chose public transportation (subway) for the poets to move from the hotel to the poetry reading venue, which is the Auditorium in the Work Training Centre of New York University. Our group of 5 authors were guided by Professor Rei Berroa to travel by subway. He happily said that since he retired from George Mason University, he has become busier with volunteer activities. He was an invitee at the 10th Americas Poetry Festival of New York, but at the same time accepted a duty to assist foreign poets in traveling and exploring around New York city. I was delighted to

Every Child lifeline /DEMO GOG international magazine

10th Americas Poetry Festival of New York

learn that he is not only a renowned professor of Spanish language and Latin American literature, but also the founder of the World Poetry Marathon, an annual event that has taken place continuously over the past 30 years.

Out of all 5 recitations and 1 roundtable discussion, I participated in 3 poetry readings. Each poet is allowed to use no more than 6 minutes at a time to read bilingual poems, in mother tongue and English. What impressed me was the simple effective organization. The ceremony was not complicated, in just 5 minutes, the Head of the Organizing Committee summarized all the results and goals of the event for 10 years. Then they focused on letting each author express themselves and their works. The main background of the event was also projected on the screen, only two standees are printed, one was placed at the entrance to the poetry reading venue, one was placed to the right of the stage, no need for flowers to decorate the stage, as well as the speaking podium. Time was carefully calculated, so that each content was presented neatly and accurately. Only the party dinners were available at the restaurant for all invitees to enjoy. We had a quick breakfast at the hotel with bread and coffee. Lunch included cakes, salads, and fried chicken wings, pre-ordered by the Organizing Committee and brought to the poetry reading site.

I saw Professor Carlos Aguasaco carry four lunch boxes for the entire invitees of the Festival in both hands, quickly walking to the subway, while talking non-stop, eyes constantly observing the authors, controlling everyone to get on and off at the correct subway station, he not only surprised me, but also gave me a new lesson on how to work and organize literary events most effectively and with the least amount of staff. During the 4 days of the event, with only 3 main members of the Organizing Committee and 2 collaborators, they took care of everything for more than 30 authors, including airport and train station transportation, accommodation, and sightseeing, poetry reading, discussion, along with taking photos, recording, and live streaming the program on Facebook, Youtube, Instagram,...

No distance, not base on position or title, all energy was focused on letting poetry's wings take off, letting authors with different languages, from different countries, express themselves and mingle in a comfortable, close atmosphere and receiving considerate care from colleagues... The organizers of the Americas Poetry Festival of New York event made me appreciate such a difference.

<u>Photos' captions:</u>
    The invitation from the 10th Americas Poetry Festival of New York to author Kieu Bich Hau
2-The author Kieu Bich Hau's image in the website of the Festival
3-The cover of the poetry book "Two moons" with 68 poems by Kieu Bich Hau (in English version) published by ArtepoeticaPress (USA) in October/2023
    4 & 5- Author Kieu Bich Hau read her poems in the Festival

Every Child lifeline /DEMO GOG international magazine

Choism in literature and art with Tamikio L. Dooley

Please introduce yourself.
Hi, my name is Tamikio L. Dooley. I'm a multi-award-winning author and poet. I write fiction, nonfiction, and children books. In my spare time, I write poetry, short stories, essays, articles, journals, and inspiring books.

How did you learn about choism and what is it in your opinion?
Alexander Kabishev, a dearest friend and fellow writer, introduced me to the concept of choism earlier this year. The concept sounded unfamiliar to me at first by different terms, but when Alexander explained the concept, I caught on. My opinion about choism, I think it's fascinating! I became interested immediately after learning the concept and the meaning of the word... very impressive.

How can choism be of interest to the author and the reader / viewer of the 21st century?
Well, since the term simply means 'choice' choism plays a huge role in the society breeding writers. Former writers can grasp the concept when understanding the word, or new writers can to the same. At the end of it all, whether we are former and uprising writers, we must grasp the term. Now, how it plays a key role for authors and readers? Authors have the 'choice' of what they want to write about such as genre, setting, plot, theme, etc. Readers have the 'choice' of what they plant in their imaginations, what they choose to read, and invite into their space.

What contribution have you made to the development of choism?
Within the little time Alexander introduced the concept of choism to me, I've written and contributed sixteen articles on the concept to our book entitled *Choism Collection of Articles*. Alexander Kabishev and I co-authored the book. I would say I understand the word very well, more than I expected. I really enjoy the research and study of the unique term.

What are the features of choism?
I'm still researching and studying all there is to know about choism, so I can't point out yet, the specific features.

How does Choism differ, for example, from surrealism or Impressionism?
The meaning of Impressionism deals with everyday matters in real life situations. This paints a style in way of life. Surrealism pretty much means the same. So, really, choism is no different than surrealism and impression. The three terms simply means 'making daily choices' in everyday life.

On the example of which artistic or literary works can we "feel" choism?
Definitely. During researching and studying choism, three of my articles written on the concept involve art. Again how does choism work? The same in 'making daily choices' in everyday life so does the artist, illustrator, or painter. Individuals with such talent must come up with what they choose to paint, what colors they choose to put in their work, style, texture, and etc. No matter what it's still a choice.

How do you see the future of choism?
I see choism in the future, for some individuals will make better choices, some people will grasp the concept of choism, while other people will reject it, still making everyday life decisions involving choism (choice).

Will you continue to develop this phenomenon? What will be your next steps in the development of this trend?
Certainly, I will continue further researching, studying, writing, and looking for ways to expand choism in various articles, essays, journals, and alternative examples.

What would you like to recommend or wish to authors who choose choism as their creative path?
I would recommend authors to get in the game! Join the choism movement. If they are afraid of the word they are familiar with, don't be afraid the grasp the concept, the meaning of the word. And certainly, don't argue with those who are teaching the concept. We learn something new every day.

Tamikio L. Dooley is an award-winning author. She is the author of 100 titles and 86 published books. The author writes fiction and nonfiction of crime, thriller, mystery, fantasy, historical, western, romance, zombie apocalypse, and paranormal. In her spare time, she writes short stories, poetry, health books, children books, diaries, journals, and inspiring books. The author is featured in Ukiyoto Publishing Litteratura, Litteratura in Paris, Itinerantur, Humanity Magazine CreatiVIngenuitiy Magazine, Kidliomag, and Connection E-Magazine. Tamikio has received awards and certificates for her short stories, poetry, articles, and essays published in Ukiyoto Publishing Anthologies, Bard's Day Key Anthology, and Multinational Pen Soldiers Anthology. Tamikio received an honorable recognition as the best crime author in September 2016, awarded the World Literary Award 2022, National Poetry Stage Bangladesh Award 2023, International Peace Medal Award, Peace Award, certificate for Hyperpoem Book (a poetry book publishing 1692 poets) "Zheng Nian Cup" National Literature (second place prize) 2023, Virtual International Artist Gallery Certificate, Best Leadership Award 2023, and won her first crystal trophy award in the crime category, and other awards.

Every Child lifeline /DEMO GOG international magazine

SOUTH AMERICA
Jorge Ducoli

Every Child lifeline /DEMO GOG international magazine

Face of the continent

Jorge Ducoli and his works in books, posts and magazines

Jorge Ducoli

Escribir a partir del dolor...

Esas son mis raíces literarias...

A los diez años falleció mi padre, escribir significaba trasladarme de la realidad y era lo único que me hacía sentir bien. Gané un concurso en el colegio y desde entonces comencé a escribir las cosas cotidianas que suceden en la vida misma, reales, y yo las trasmito a mi manera.

Muchas veces vuela mi imaginación y surgen, creo, cosas hermosas, quizás tristes pero bonitas. Amo la poesía, soy un romántico sin cura y siento que al transmitir mis escritos, por lo que me llega, ayudo a superar sin darme cuenta a las personas que muchas veces con lo que escribo se sienten identificadas y siempre digo:

No soy poeta, no soy escritor,

soy un loco soñador

que más allá de su cordura

se desvela por amor,

más allá de la locura

hermosa locura de amor....

163

Quien pudiera

Para mi querida amiga Nora Medes

Quien pudiera detener el tiempo,
horas, minutos, segundos,
de los momentos felices de nuestras vidas.
Quien pudiera borrar
los malos momentos pasados
que ni siquiera sean recuerdos.
Quien pudiera amar y ser amado,
detenerse en tiempo y espacio
amarrados a algo tan hermoso
como es el amor, yo lo haría,
para que cada persona que conozco,
esté libre de sufrimientos.
Pero no puedo, si existe alguien bienvenido sea
sino seguiré con la esperanza de una vida mejor,
luchando por lo único que me mantiene vivo,
el amor, hacia mi familia, amigos,
seres queridos que ya no están,
esperando volver a verlos algún día,
eso sí puedo hacerlo,
lo demás ...quien pudiera.

En ti encontré un remanso de agua clara, contenciones caricias y besos, alejandome de las turbulencias de la vida, trasladandome a otro mundo un nuevo universo donde logro escapar de la soledad que me golpea sin piedad al transcurso de los años la necesidad de morir entre sus brazos hoy de vivir entre los tuyos, amandote, temiendote, cuidandote en las mansas aguas de tu cuerpo.
Jorge Duc

Di mi nombre, mira al cielo

Para mi hija Sofía

Sin conocerte te amaba
orgullo felicidad sentí
la primer vez que te vi
fuera del vientre materno.

Siendo mi vida un infierno
sin proyectos, sin futuro,
sos la bendición te aseguro
por ti sigo viviendo,
es tan grande el amor que siento
difícil de explicar,
lo puedo demostrar
a medida que estas creciendo.

Hija mía no te miento
cuenta conmigo hasta el final,
el día que no esté más
di mi nombre mira al cielo,
encontrarás el consuelo
de algún modo acudiré,
contigo siempre estaré
para calmar tus lamentos.

163

Every Child lifeline /DEMO GOG international magazine

Free microphone

Amb. Dra. H.C. Maria Elena Ramirez
The Mystical Muse Of Poetry

"POETRY NOTES"

"In the white pages
seal with the pen
falls at my feet every
tomorrow a recital
of letters with wings
angels singing
verses captured
with lyrics that encourage
hands on a
dusty piano,
Illuminating dreams when writing
poetry notes, singing,
that resonate slowly
from the soul, the essence
divine of this
muse declaiming,
communication that carries
messages of peace to the world
through the word
steps of glory spread
harmony to brother peoples,
connect with culture
eradicating the violence that
transcend by giant steps
this endless number of emotions
of Angels and Archangels praying,
soon humanity awakens
will sing with white flags
crying out for peace."

THE CHILDREN OF THE WORLD

the color of the days
they paint the sky with
white doves and
children admiring
nature and
little things that
life gives you.
The peace of the world
is built with
a smile when
dawns and remains
the soul of the happy child
and transmits to humanity
that calm
The night comes and its happiness
full at the end of a day together
his hands and begins with
prayer thanking God,
for the day that has repaired him.

Every Child lifeline /DEMO GOG international magazine

Free microphone

IS THIS WHAT THEY CALL LOVE?

He was born and smiled.
He discovered a new world with amazement,
his mother's smile greeted him,
What alchemy transforms pain into love?
Will it be the first lesson he learned?
the lost word in dark matter,
in the maze of life,
love?
The fledgling stonemason who cuts his stone,
spattering his cloak with rubble,
wounding unconscious, his own hand,
filling his eyes with scum,
turning them red,
filling them with tears,
but by his side he feels patient; without anger,
the companion and teacher: his brother,
to teach him how to shape his stone,
protecting it from the stubble,
covering him with his apron,
Is this what they call love?
He doesn't avert his eyes
of the man who stretches out his hand,
among the souls that come and go,
who extends his hand asking for a piece of bread,
Among the garden where once stood an apple tree,
Is this what they call love?
 fight daily with the fierce chimera,
that burns the man who believes in absolute reason
Could it be that you believe that freedom is the same as love?
Could it be that he senses the same chimera that strikes with his dragon legs? ,
He keeps fighting because he believes that his heart has its own conviction,
Gentlemen I want to know:
Is this what they call love?
He, on his lips, always has a smile drawn,
in his hands that give without waiting he has a song,
He feels his breeze on his face from the stars,
and feeds on the honey of forgiveness,
without hesitation he covers the naked with his shirt,
recognizes his siblings as such
combs the hair of wise Artemis,
And recognize THE ALL and love as one,
like the great immortal.
Is this what they call love?
God I want to know
Why am I feeling a magnet inside of me?
my two opposite poles repudiating each other,
but powerfully attracted to each other,
with the force of a sledgehammer,
with the strength of God,
and his arm,
Plunging a chisel deep inside of me
Is this what they call love?
Answer please

RODOLFO ZAMORA COREA
BIOGRAPHY

Writer and poet born February 14, 1966, in Nicaragua, based in Costa Rica.
His poems have been translated into Vietnamese, Arabic, English, Italian, Romanian among other world languages.
• Read in more than 50 countries around the world and with more than 10 literary works and dozens of international recognitions.
• Publishes with major literary groups in Asia, Europe, Australia, Africa, and the Americas including the United States.
• His works can be read virtually in the virtual library of Stanford University, Harvard University, Yale, University of New Mexico, New York University, among others, as well as in the virtual Library of Congress of the United States of America, Library of the Bank Central de Nicaragua and WORLD CAT-OCLC considered the largest online catalog in the world.

Every Child lifeline /DEMO GOG international magazine

Face of the continent

Sensation From The Heart is a compilation of wonderful family members of United Poets @ Heart (UPAH) where we truly expresses our deepest emotions in terms of love..It's the epitome of one person innersoul and a knowledge of gaining power through heartaches and wins in life..We aim to let the world see our kindness heart to inspire and loves us by many to support our mission and vision and empower more who dwell on suffered from anything..The unity of our quills provoke the assurance of our sincerity and enthusiasm to be the better version of ourselves...

Ms. Veronica Roma Pingol hails from Dasmariñas, Cavite, Philippines. She is a Filipina blessed with a beautiful daughter named Louella. Currently, she resides in Hong Kong as an empowered woman and serves as the founder of United Poets @ Heart, a poetry platform on Facebook with a membership exceeding thousands. Veronica is also the author of her debut solo book, titled "Night Butterfly," a reflection on life, love, and the soul, now available worldwide. In addition to her writing pursuits, Veronica is a child advisor for the Glory Future Foundation in Bangladesh. Her dedication involves supporting children in need and working towards the foundation's goals. Furthermore, she serves as an International Editor for Migospecta, Homagi, Christian Global magazines, and journals. Veronica has been featured across multiple multimedia platforms, including television, radio, newspapers, websites, magazines, and various book anthologies. Veronica's optimistic character and attitude have garnered recognition and praise, as she stays true to herself while positively impacting others. Her life has been marked by failures and struggles, yet they have not deterred her from pushing forward, maintaining a smile, and understanding the ebb and flow of life. She finds solace in music, singing, dancing, and writing, while the sea serves as her sanctuary, a place of relaxation where she rejuvenates herself before penning remarkable poems. With her adventurous nature, Veronica actively participates in diverse activities as a leader, public figure, and author, leaving a lasting impression. As a responsible citizen and multitasker, Veronica continuously seeks personal growth and exploration in her quest for happiness and contentment, molding her into the bold individual she is today. Connecting with others, delving into their stories, and reading their poems enables Veronica to express her empathy towards those who are emotionally downtrodden or feel hopeless. Through her poetry, she hopes to touch hearts and convey the love she holds within. This second book is priceless to Veronica, as it serves as a medium to express and spread her genuine emotions during that period. Her ultimate desire is to create a better world for everyone, encouraging confidence in embracing the realities of life and fostering optimism without prejudice. Veronica's famous words of wisdom encapsulate her philosophy: "Chase your dreams, work for them, be yourself, and strive to become the best version of yourself."

Every Child lifeline /DEMO GOG international magazine

Free microphone

Mildred DJ. Par is a poetess from the Philippines. A former college lecturer teaching Research and Literature for more than 20 years, she has also been published in many international anthologies and publications including both magazines and newspapers in different countries on both online and offline. Currently, she is teaching 21st Century Literature and Practical Research in Senior High school.

Life is Beautiful

Do not complain
Life in this world is harsh
It simply won't change.
Onward, on in its diurnal pace
Our lives just go with the flow.
It won't stop, nor care
Even if you dare.

But people often
Mismanage their lives
Soon, they grumble.
Life is difficult, full of pain.
Once you err, you suffer.
The road to recovery
May not always be easy.

Therefore, reach out
In prayers, learn to surrender.
Don't be too proud.
We don't have any control
of the design, of the system.
Be grateful for the life we live
Life is what we make it
Life is beautiful.

8 July 2023
Philippines

Every Child lifeline /DEMO GOG international magazine

Free microphone

Divine-rest

You may feel ice-cold death
Don't be scared
It's right next to you
And caring for you silently
No one knew
No one even noticed
You existed
and you will remain here forever
You will free us
and you will arrange a divinely secured shelter
leaving this noisy crowd
In a vast forest
next to the beautiful fountain on the hill
Peaceful rest in divine nature
Moments with a strange sound in the melodious wind
Then a familiar voice from far away
falling asleep again
After a while, whispering
Let's have a look your new place
A place of peace and light
A beautiful secured shelter
Your soul reaches to your loved one
Asleep or awake
You are gradually more intimate
A beautiful soulmate
All your memories are alive
All unfinished work is on the way to the destination
Your love has reached all
Your indifference is on another level today
The old house surrounded by your emptiness;
newly lighted
and more presence of your loved ones there
May you rest in peace
And spread your light among travelers.

16/03/2022
Western australia

A lover of art, culture, and humanity, she aims for her readers to resonate with her stories. Her work is published on multiple platforms in English, Bengali, Oria/Odia and Spanish. Creative writing is a breath of fresh air for her, and she wishes her readers will feel the same. Her first Bengali poetry book was published in 2021.

Moly Siddiqua is a Bangladeshi Australian poetess and living in Western Australia. She studied Human Rights and currently she is working at the Australian Government. Writing is her passion and she wants to continue this journey for peace and unity.

Every Child lifeline / DEMO GOG international magazine

Free microphone

"Sonny Perida's Colorful and Natural Artworld"
By Elizabeth Esguerra Castillo

"They say that for as long as there has been art, artists have been enthused by nature."

Sonny's early exposure to the Arts stemmed from his Father's automotive shop where he started designing Pinoy jeepneys. Perida took up a Bachelor of Fine Arts Major in Advertising degree at the Far Eastern University and was influenced by his friends, colleagues, and contemporaries at the Group Artist of Taytay (GAT) where he was also a member.

A nature lover by heart, Perida gets inspiration from Mother Nature and his beautiful surroundings. Let us just say that he "sees the beauty in everything". This is evidently depicted in his masterpieces in which he incorporates environmental and natural elements. It is no wonder his artworks were created in rich and colorful tones for he admires and looks up to Filipino National Artist Fernando Amorsolo, the Realist Painter who is known for his application of natural lighting in his paintings.

Depictions of nature in one's art can also be about intellectual thought, spirituality, and higher consciousness. Art involving nature can be done simply to display the beauty of the natural world around us, to make scientific observations in an environment, or to open our minds to philosophical ideas about our own connection to nature and beyond.

Looking closely at his artworks, one just can't help but get hypnotized by their magnificence.

The Global Pinoy Artist is not just adept in painting but as well as in creating brilliant murals, sculptures, and designs. Perida's designs have been used in public utility jeepneys, visual displays in stores, and in labels of merchandise of Viva Video Incorporated in the Philippines.

He presently works as a Product Art Designer in China and devotes most of his free time to creating his next masterpiece. Perida is also member of Artipolo Group in Antipolo City, Philippines, and FilEstilo in Guangdong, China.

Every Child lifeline /DEMO GOG international magazine

Free microphone

Here is our short interview with the talented artist so you can get to know him better:

1. When did you discover that you have an inclination to the Arts? Was it when you were younger or later on in life?

Answer: At a tender age of 12 years old, I was already helping my father with our family business in our automotive shop where I started designing jeepney arts. I began discovering my inclination to the Arts with the help of my Ninong Jun Santillan, who taught me a lot of things in making designs in arts and inspired me in this field.

2. How can you describe your art style?

Answer: As for me, I'll love the way of the old traditional style of painting Realism.
 I was deeply inspired by nature and the environment and
  living things around me, in my eyes I love the detailing of these images
  in the natural world and environmental elements enable me to create
  fascinating masterpieces using acrylic or oil on canvas as medium in which I apply rich tones to give viewers a vivid representation of nature.

3. Do you still have plans of exploring other art genres or to learn about other art styles?

Answer: Yes, I do have plans of exploring other art genres such as Surrealism and
 Abstract these art genres are my second target for I want to develop & explore them more
 in the near future.

4. Who among the famous painters do you look up to and why?

Answer: For Realist Artists, I admire National Artist Fernando Amorsolo the most because I love the colors he used & natural lighting and backlighting in his paintings, which made him famous. For Surrealism, I admire Salvador Dali because of his technical skill, precise draftsmanship, and the striking, bizarre images in his work which made him more unique and well-known.

5. What can you say to the young and aspiring Filipino artists?

Answer: All I can say to the young & aspiring Filipino Artist: "Don't stop dreaming keep on believing in yourself the more you, do the more you explore.
 "You must trust your own madness in this field."

Every Child lifeline /DEMO GOG international magazine

CHRISTOS DIKBASANIS
ANTARCTICA

Every Child lifeline /DEMO GOG international magazine

Face of the continent

LIFE WITHOUT SUN

How long has it been from
the last check in of my life
and now she is lost
in the snowy landscapes
of Antarctic's land?
How my youth slipped
between my fingers,
as I was engrossed
from futile experiments
and new discoveries that ensnared my life?
The snow now gives me no more time
Only in the past
it allows me to gallop
like a deer in the white landscape
I have already lost my life
in the endless night
who succeeds her for a while
a Sun sick and helpless
Antarctic's sun
which has wrapped
in his swaddling clothes
my dayless life.

BIOGRAPHY
CHRISTOS DIKBASANIS is a poet, writer and scholar of religions. He was born in Thessaloniki, Greece, where he graduated from the Theological School of the Aristotle University. He holds a Master's Degree from the Theological School with a specialization in Religious Studies. It has also been included in the "Great Encyclopedia of Mondern Greek Literature" of Haris Patsi publications and in the "Who's Who" of journalists. He has been honored with many national and international awards for his poems.

Every Child lifeline /DEMO GOG international magazine

Free microphone

Estate

L'aria è un abbaglio d'intensità lucente
sui litorali - l'azzurrità del mare -
si lega ai pascoli del cielo,
s'umetta il volto di madido salato.
Gongola il vento un bendidio
d'alchemico mistero, l'afa agostana
- fiacca - la volontà di fare
col solleone divampano gli incendi
nelle città - l'asfalto insofferente
ustiona passi d'animale.
Un altro mondo nel cuore delle Alpi
tutto pare rinascere tra gli astri,
il fresco alito dei monti
ammalia corpo e anima di tregua
lo scampanio dei greggi
è un cantico di grazia.
Fugge lontano il vagabondo eco
di cicale
l'occhio steso su erbosi tratti di bonaccia
fatica a sporgersi all'indietro,
un delicato soffio scompiglia
ricordi teneri d'infanzia,
l'estate tra le alture è angelico diletto.

S'invera un'estasi solare

Nel limbo nebuloso s'invera un'estasi solare
l'affanno delle onde
di vivido sussulto invalida l'abbiocco,
- vello d'ambrata sabbia -
la pelle s'accoccola di bronzo,
ogni colore è musa d'euforia.
Su liquidi cristalli s'assiepano i gabbiani
- scogli anneriti di mitili aggrappati -
un gioco d'acque mosse spruzza salsedine sui volti
stelle marine ingioiano di cielo la battigia.
Nell'agorà dei sensi impazza un tempo di vermiglio
all'orizzonte l'estate è complice d'amore.

A solar ecstasy comes true

In the nebulous limbo a solar ecstasy waxes
the breathlessness of the waves
of vivid gasps invalidates the drowsiness,
- fleece of amber sand -
the skin snuggles with bronze,
every color is muse of euphoria.
On liquid crystals throng the seagulls
- blackened reefs of clinging mussels –
a play of choppy waters splashes saltiness on faces
starfish bejewel the shoreline with sky.
In the agora of the senses rages a time of vermilion
on the horizon summer is love's accomplice.

Manuela Cecchetti, author of essays and poems, is a graduate in Religious Studies and a member of the Camerata dei Poeti in Florence. In 2019 she published La terra... un pianeta da amare. Changing mentalities and adopting new lifestyles for an economy of well-being (Il Ponte Vecchio), preface by Monsignor Erio Castellucci. March 2022 saw the publication of his new essay The Greatest Human Being of the 20th Century. La straordinaria vicenda di Albert Schweitzer (Bertoni), contribution by Mariella Enoc, preface by Angela Ales Bello, introduction by Franco Cardini, afterword by Eric Noffke. In September 2022, he published his first poetry collection Lampi Bagliori Diamanti. Meteore d'Eterno (Ensemble), preface by Anna Santoliquido and afterword by Nazario Pardini. In May 2023, his latest poetic collection Crepuscoli d'aurora - preface by poet and literary critic Carmelo Consoli, president of the 'Camerata dei Poeti di Firenze' - was released in bookshops. Some of his unpublished works have been published on the website of the well-known magazine 'Nuovi Argomenti', founded in 1953 by Alberto Carocci and Alberto Moravia, and currently directed by the illustrious writer Dacia Maraini.

Every Child lifeline / DEMO GOG international magazine
Information page and our team

Chief editor: Alexander Kabishev

Consultant editor: Collins Osinachi Emeghara

World Secretary: Milica Boskovic

Consultant editor: Dervisa Colakovic

Asia and Europe Direction Editor: Ana Stjelja

Consultant editor: Kieu Bich Hau

Greece Direction Editor: Xanthi Hondrou

Oceania Direction Editor: Elizabeth Esguerra Castillo

Direction Editor Serbia (SCOR Union): Miloš Ivetić

Direction Editor Serbia (SCOR Union): Maria Jotich

Author of the article: Souad Khalil

Assistant Designer: Dessy Tsvetkova

Assistant editor: Ifigenia Metochi

Editor from the Union RRM3: Franca Colozzo

Editor from the Union RRM3: George Onsy

Consultant editor: Svetozar Rakic

Editor of the Italian direction: Lidia Chiarelli

Consultant editor: Cvija Peranovic

South America Direction Editor: Victoria Helena Rios

Turkey Direction Editor: Türkan Ergör

www.ingramcontent.com/pod-product-compliance
Lightning Source LLC
LaVergne TN
LVHW061945070526
838199LV00060B/3981